TEEN CHEF *Cooks*

TEEN CHEF *Cooks*

FOOD NETWORK'S
CHOPPED TEEN
GRAND CHAMPION

★

Eliana de Las Casas

80
SCRUMPTIOUS,
FAMILY-FRIENDLY
RECIPES

RODALE
BOOKS

New York

Published in the United States by Rodale Books,
an imprint of Random House, a division of
Penguin Random House LLC, New York.

rodalebooks.com

RODALE and the Plant colophon are registered
trademarks of Penguin Random House LLC.

Library of Congress Cataloging-in-Publication
Data is available upon request.

ISBN 978-1-63565-194-2
Ebook ISBN 978-1-6365-195-9

Printed in China

Book design by Francesca Truman
Photographs by Mitch Mandel

10 9 8 7 6 5 4 3 2 1

First Edition

In memory of my mom,
Dianne de Las Casas.
Thank you for supporting my journey
from the very beginning.
I love you times infinity infinities!

Contents

Introduction

My journey into the kitchen began when I was four years old. I was drawn to the smell of the food, and I asked my mom if I could help her cook. She gave me a step stool, and I mixed the potatoes in the pan as she watched over me very carefully. When the potatoes were finished cooking, I was so excited for my dad and sister to taste what I had helped my mom make. We served them our dish, and they ate every last bit. Ever since that moment, you can always find me in the kitchen with my apron and chef's hat on, cooking up a storm.

I come from an international family of cooks, which means that our dinner table is always filled with global delicacies. My nana is Filipina, my paw paw is Cajun, my abuela is Honduran, and my papi was Cuban. These culinary influencers, along with my growing up in New Orleans, contributed to my passion for cooking. In New Orleans, we don't eat to live—we live to eat. We bond over our love for food but also debate whose grandma makes the best gumbo. And whether it's deciding what new restaurant to eat at or where to get a good king cake, our conversations always end up being about food.

I graduated from the New Orleans Center for Creative Arts (NOCCA), a high school arts conservatory with a full four-year culinary arts program funded, in part, by the Emeril Lagasse Foundation with a Johnson & Wales curriculum. Some of our culinary training included working in Press Street Gardens, an urban farm used for teaching NOCCA students and educating the public about gardening and nutrition. There we seeded, planted, and harvested many different varieties of produce. We also raised chickens, goats, and ducks.

For many years, I have been working with the Crescent City Farmers Market as their Marketeer Ambassador. In this capacity, I shop the market for what is fresh and in season, invent a recipe on the spot, and cook it for the hungry, anticipating crowd. My favorite part about doing cooking demonstrations at the market is when people who are reluctant to try new foods taste my dishes and love them. My samples always run out, and people are inspired to buy the seasonal produce to re-create my recipes.

In my backyard at home, I have my own kitchen garden. I grow many types of herbs, including basil, oregano, thyme, mint, sage, chives, and rosemary. I like to plant different fruits and vegetables such as strawberries, blueberries, bell peppers, jalapeños, carrots, squash, arugula, and lettuce. I even have an orange and a lemon tree. My nana and abuela also have gardens and often supply me with fresh fruit, veggies, and herbs from their surplus crops. I love being able to pop right into my backyard to select ingredients for whatever meal I'm cooking.

This book's recipes are divided by season: spring, summer, fall, and winter. There are lists on pages 14–15 showing what produce is commonly grown during each season. The recipes correspond to many of the fruits, veggies, and herbs. When you shop at your grocery store, look for produce that is grown locally. Produce that is local and in season is always the freshest and tastiest.

From my garden to your table, I hope you enjoy these recipes and are inspired to cook fresh and seasonally.

Bon appétit! Let's eat!

In-Season
Produce

Spring

- APPLE
- APRICOT
- ARUGULA
- ASPARAGUS
- AVOCADO
- BANANA
- BROCCOLI
- CABBAGE
- CARROT
- CELERY
- CILANTRO
- GARLIC
- KALE
- LETTUCE
- MANGO
- MUSHROOM
- ONION
- PEAS
- PINEAPPLE
- POTATO
- RADISH
- RHUBARB
- SPINACH
- STRAWBERRY
- TURNIP

Summer

- APPLE
- APRICOT
- AVOCADO
- BANANA
- BANANA PEPPER
- BASIL
- BEET
- BELL PEPPER
- BLACKBERRY
- BLUEBERRY
- CARROT
- CELERY
- CHERRY
- COLLARD GREEN
- CORN
- CUCUMBER
- EGGPLANT
- GARLIC
- GREEN BEAN
- KIWI
- LIMA BEAN
- MANGO
- MELON
- NECTARINE
- OKRA
- PEACH
- PLUM
- RASPBERRY
- STRAWBERRY
- SUMMER SQUASH
- TOMATILLO
- TOMATO
- ZUCCHINI

Fall

APPLE
BANANA
BEET
BELL PEPPER
BROCCOLI
BRUSSELS SPROUT
CABBAGE
CARROT
CAULIFLOWER
CELERY
CORN
CRANBERRY
GARLIC
GINGER
GRAPES
GREEN BEAN
KALE
LEMON
LETTUCE
MANGO
MUSHROOM
ONION
PARSNIP
PEA
PEAR
PINEAPPLE
POTATO
PUMPKIN
RADISH
RASPBERRY
RUTABAGA
SPINACH
SWEET POTATO
TURNIP
WINTER SQUASH
YAM
ZUCCHINI

⚜

Winter

APPLE
AVOCADO
BANANA
BEET
BRUSSELS SPROUT
BUTTERNUT SQUASH
CABBAGE
CARROT
CELERY
KALE
KUMQUAT
LEEK
LEMON
ONION
ORANGE
PARSNIP
PEAR
PINEAPPLE
POMEGRANATE
POMELO
POTATO
PUMPKIN
RUTABAGA
SWEET POTATO
TURNIP
YAM

⚜

Spring

Turnip au Gratin

2 tablespoons olive oil

¼ cup chopped shallot

2 garlic cloves, minced

1 tablespoon all-purpose flour

2 cups heavy cream

1 teaspoon sea salt

½ teaspoon ground white pepper

1 cup grated mozzarella cheese

3 large turnips, thinly sliced

2 cups chopped Swiss chard leaves

2 cups grated Gruyère cheese

6 tablespoons panko bread crumbs

Au gratin is a French technique of covering a dish with cheese and bread crumbs and baking it, resulting in a golden brown top layer. What's lovely about au gratins is that you can use any in-season vegetables. This recipe was created with ingredients from my local farmer's market. You could use radishes instead of turnips because they have a similar earthy flavor. Or you could make a classic potato au gratin.

1. Preheat the oven to 375°F.

2. In a medium pot, heat the oil over medium heat. Add the shallot and cook, stirring frequently, for 5 minutes, or until translucent. Stir in the garlic and cook for 30 seconds. Add the flour, heavy cream, salt, and white pepper, reduce the heat to medium-low and cook for 5 minutes, or until the sauce begins to thicken. Stir in the mozzarella until it melts and remove from the heat.

3. In an 8-inch square casserole dish, begin layering the ingredients. Place a layer of turnips (1 sliced turnip) over the bottom. Cover the turnip layer with a handful of the chard. Pour one-third of the cheese sauce on top. Sprinkle with 2 tablespoons of the bread crumbs. Repeat the layers twice more, ending with the cheese sauce and the bread crumbs on the very top. Cover with aluminum foil and bake for 55 minutes, then switch the oven to broil. Remove the foil and broil for 3 to 5 minutes, until the cheese sauce bubbles and the bread crumbs turn golden brown.

4. Let the turnip au gratin cool and set for 15 minutes before serving.

Coffee-Grilled Pork Tenderloin with *Apple*-Vanilla Compote

❧ SERVES 4
PREP TIME: 40 MIN
COOK TIME: 30 MIN

TENDERLOIN

2 tablespoons ground coffee

2 tablespoons packed light brown sugar

1 teaspoon smoked paprika

½ teaspoon ground chipotle chile

½ teaspoon sea salt

1 (3-pound) pork tenderloin

COMPOTE

2 Granny Smith apples, peeled, cored, and chopped (2 cups)

1½ tablespoons packed light brown sugar

1 teaspoon pure vanilla extract

½ teaspoon ground cinnamon

¼ teaspoon freshly grated nutmeg

1 tablespoon torn fresh mint leaves

A food company once mailed me a box of their products and asked me to use those products to invent a recipe they could share with their customers. I created this dish because I loved the idea of using the company's coffee to make a rub. The combination of the sweet compote with the smoky, coffee-infused tenderloin is so delicious that you'll want to go back for seconds.

1. **For the tenderloin:** In a small bowl, mix the coffee, brown sugar, paprika, chipotle, and salt. Place the tenderloin on a plate or baking dish. Rub the mixture onto the tenderloin, cover with plastic wrap, and let sit in the refrigerator for 30 minutes.

2. Heat a grill to medium-high (400°F).

3. **For the compote:** In a medium saucepan, combine the apples, brown sugar, vanilla, cinnamon, nutmeg, and ½ cup water. Cook over medium-low heat for 15 minutes, or until the water has completely evaporated and the apples are tender. Remove from heat and stir in the mint.

4. Grill the tenderloin over direct heat, turning it often, for 25 to 30 minutes, until a thermometer inserted into the thickest portion registers 145°F. Set the pork on a cutting board to rest for 5 minutes.

5. Slice the pork and serve it with the compote alongside.

Skillet Lasagne with *Arugula*

❧ SERVES 8
PREP TIME: 10 MIN
COOK TIME: 30 MIN

8 ounces lasagna noodles, broken into quarters

2 tablespoons olive oil

1 yellow onion, chopped

2 garlic cloves, minced

1 pound ground beef

2 cups chopped kale leaves

1 cup arugula

¼ cup chopped garlic chives (regular chives also work)

3 cups diced tomatoes

1 tablespoon honey

2 tablespoons Creole seasoning

½ teaspoon sea salt

2 cups grated mild cheddar cheese

½ cup grated Asiago cheese

½ cup arugula flowers (optional)

2 scallions, chopped

I developed this lasagne recipe for a cooking demo at the Crescent City Farmers Market, and it was later featured in a food magazine in South Africa! Because it's made in a skillet on the stovetop, it is a wonderful time saver. Normally, you'd have to bake a lasagne for about an hour, but this stovetop method cuts your cooking time in half. If you don't have Creole seasoning, you can use 2 tablespoons Italian seasoning, 1 teaspoon paprika, and ½ teaspoon cayenne pepper in its place.

1. Bring a large pot of water to a boil. Add the lasagna noodles and cook according to the package directions. Drain and set aside.

2. Meanwhile, in a large pot, heat the olive oil over medium-high heat. Add the onion and cook, stirring frequently, for 5 minutes, until translucent. Stir in the garlic and cook for 30 seconds. Add the ground beef and cook, stirring, for 10 minutes, or until browned. Stir in the kale, arugula, garlic chives, tomatoes, honey, Creole seasoning, and salt and cook for 10 minutes, or until the tomatoes have cooked down and the kale and arugula have wilted. Keep the sauce on low heat while assembling the lasagne.

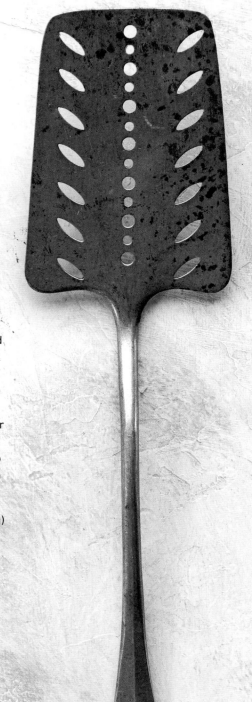

3. Set a 10-inch cast-iron skillet over medium heat. Ladle 1 cup of the meat sauce into the pan and spread it to cover the bottom evenly. Evenly sprinkle ¾ cup of the cheddar over the sauce. Arrange enough lasagna noodles on top of the cheese layer to cover it completely. Spread 1 cup of the sauce over the noodles and sprinkle with ¾ cup of the cheddar. Cover with another layer of noodles. Spread the remaining sauce over the noodles. Sprinkle the remaining ½ cup cheddar and the Asiago evenly over top. Remove from the heat and let set for 10 minutes before serving.

4. Garnish the lasagne with the arugula flowers (if using) and scallions and serve directly from the skillet.

Spinach and Asiago Strata

✤ SERVES 8
PREP TIME: 10 MIN
COOK TIME: 30 MIN

2 tablespoons olive oil

½ cup crumbled cooked sausage

3 cups fresh spinach

2 garlic cloves, minced

6 slices stale bread, cut into cubes

3 large eggs

½ cup whole milk

¼ cup heavy cream

½ cup grated Asiago cheese

1 teaspoon Creole seasoning

½ teaspoon freshly grated nutmeg

½ teaspoon sea salt

¼ teaspoon ground pepper

3 tablespoons mascarpone cheese

A strata is like a savory bread pudding. You start with a base of stale bread, eggs, and milk, then add whatever fillings you like. You can even utilize leftovers for the filling. Stratas are really great to make for breakfast. You can assemble it the night before and store it in the refrigerator. In the morning, all you have to do is pop it in the oven and enjoy.

1. Preheat the oven to 400°F.

2. In a 10-inch cast-iron skillet, heat the oil over medium-high heat. Add the sausage and heat through, about 3 minutes. Add the spinach and garlic and cook for 4 to 5 minutes, until the spinach has wilted. Turn off the heat. Stir in the bread.

3. In a medium bowl, whisk together the eggs, milk, cream, Asiago, Creole seasoning, nutmeg, salt, and white pepper. Pour the egg mixture into the skillet and press down on the bread so it absorbs all the liquid. Let sit for 5 minutes. Dollop the mascarpone over the top. Bake for 15 minutes, until the top is golden brown and the mascarpone has melted.

Sweet-and-Spicy Stir-Fried *Asparagus*

SERVES 4
PREP TIME: 5 MIN
COOK TIME: 10 MIN

1 tablespoon low-sodium soy sauce

1 tablespoon packed light brown sugar

½ teaspoon sea salt

½ teaspoon red pepper flakes

1 teaspoon toasted sesame oil

1 bunch asparagus, tough ends trimmed

Many people overcook their vegetables, especially when blanching or steaming them. They end up with a soggy mess. Cooking vegetables in a wok on high heat for a shorter amount of time eliminates that problem. I love how the asparagus still has a bit of a crunch when I bite into it. It also has just the right amount of heat, with a little sweetness to balance it out.

1. In a small bowl, stir together the soy sauce, sugar, salt, and red pepper flakes. Set aside.

2. In a wok or large skillet, heat the sesame oil over high heat. Add the asparagus and cook, stirring frequently, for 8 minutes. Pour the soy sauce mixture over the asparagus and cook, stirring continuously, for 2 minutes, or until the asparagus has slightly softened. Serve immediately.

Avocado Fries
with Sriracha Sour Cream

⚜ SERVES 8
PREP TIME: 10 MIN
COOK TIME: 10 MIN

FRIES

4 avocados, halved and pitted, but not peeled

3 cups panko bread crumbs

½ cup Parmesan cheese

2 teaspoons sea salt

1 teaspoon ground white pepper

4 large eggs

Nonstick cooking spray

SRIRACHA SOUR CREAM

1 cup sour cream

2 teaspoons sriracha

FOR SERVING

¼ cup crumbled queso fresco

A friend of mine who loves french fries asked me to create a lighter option for him. I came up with these avocado fries, and he devoured them. With this recipe, you get the same crunch effect that you would have with a crispy french fry, but with a creamy inside that just melts in your mouth. Dip it in the sriracha sour cream and you have spice, too. It all works so well together. Plus, who doesn't love avocados?

1. **For the fries:** Preheat the oven to 400°F. Set a wire rack in a rimmed baking sheet.

2. Slice the avocados into thick wedges and remove the skin from each wedge.

3. In a medium bowl, stir together the panko bread crumbs, Parmesan, salt, and white pepper. Put the eggs in a medium bowl and beat with a fork. Dip the avocado wedges in the egg, letting any excess drip off, then coat them with the bread crumbs. Place the breaded avocado wedges on the prepared rack and spray with cooking spray. Bake for 10 minutes, or until golden brown and crispy.

4. **For the sriracha sour cream:** In a small bowl, thoroughly mix the sour cream and sriracha.

5. Top the fries with the queso fresco and serve with the sriracha sour cream alongside.

Avocado Fries with
Sriracha Sour Cream
PAGE 27

Roasted *Broccoli* with Smoked Sausage

3 cups broccoli florets

4 tablespoons olive oil

1 teaspoon sea salt

¼ cup chopped yellow onion

2 garlic cloves, minced

12 ounces smoked sausages, cut crosswise into ½-inch-thick slices

I love roasting vegetables because it brings out their natural sweetness. It is so simple to toss veggies in olive oil, season them, and pop them into the oven. If you have a heavier main meal, this is the perfect accompaniment as a side dish. You can also make this recipe vegan by using plant-based smoked sausage—it tastes just like the regular version!

1. Preheat the oven to 400°F. Line a baking sheet with aluminum foil.

2. Spread the broccoli over the prepared baking sheet and coat with 2 tablespoons of the oil and the salt. Roast for 20 minutes, or until golden brown and fork-tender.

3. In a large pan, heat the remaining 2 tablespoons oil over medium heat. Add the onion and cook, stirring frequently, for 3 to 5 minutes, until translucent. Stir in the garlic and cook for 30 seconds. Add the smoked sausage and cook for 5 minutes, or until browned. Stir in the broccoli and cook for 1 minute more.

Latin Slaw with *Cilantro*

✦ SERVES 10
PREP TIME: 1 HR 10 MIN
COOK TIME: 0 MIN

2 cups packaged slaw mix

1 tablespoon fresh lime juice

1 tablespoon Greek yogurt

1 teaspoon distilled white vinegar

1 teaspoon finely chopped jalapeño

1 tablespoon chopped fresh cilantro

½ teaspoon sea salt

¼ teaspoon ground black pepper

¼ teaspoon ground cumin

¼ teaspoon paprika

I created this recipe for a charity event I do every year called the Azúcar Ball. I decided to make the slaw with Greek yogurt because I've never been a fan of coleslaw made with mayonnaise. Once I tasted the slaw, it became a staple taco topper in my house. This recipe is great for large family gatherings or parties because it makes so much slaw. I like setting up a taco bar with tortillas, meat, and toppings so everyone can make their own tacos and top them however they please.

In a large bowl, stir together the slaw mix, lime juice, yogurt, vinegar, jalapeño, cilantro, salt, pepper, cumin, and paprika. Cover and refrigerate for 1 hour. Serve cold.

Lemongrass-Plum Oyster *Mushrooms*

1 tablespoon toasted sesame oil

2 shallots, minced

2 garlic cloves, minced

2 cups oyster mushrooms, stems removed

1 plum, pitted and chopped

1 tablespoon lemongrass paste

1 tablespoon soy sauce

Chopped cilantro, for garnish

This is a great side dish to whip up if you're in a hurry. Combining sweet fruit, citrusy lemongrass, and savory oyster mushrooms makes for an unusual but satisfying combo. If you can't find lemongrass paste, you can use fresh lemongrass. Cut the top and bottom off the stalk, then slice it lengthwise down the center and peel away the hard outer layers so you're left with just the tender inside. Finely chop the lemongrass and use it in the recipe in place of the lemongrass paste.

1. In a medium pan, heat the oil over medium heat. Add the shallots and cook, stirring frequently, for 3 to 5 minutes, until translucent. Stir in the garlic and cook for 30 seconds. Add the mushrooms and plum and cook for 5 minutes. Add the lemongrass and soy sauce and cook, stirring, for 3 minutes, or until the sauce begins to thicken.

2. Serve the mushrooms garnished with the cilantro.

Honey-Roasted *Carrot* Strips

PREP TIME: 15 MIN
COOK TIME: 25 MIN

1 (32-ounce) bag rainbow carrots,
or 8 large rainbow carrots

½ teaspoon sea salt

½ cup (1 stick) unsalted butter, melted

⅓ cup honey

Rainbow carrots jazz up this dish with lots of color. When I first created this recipe, I made it for our big Easter brunch. I took the roasted carrots and arranged them in the shape of a bird's nest on a platter. Then I placed hard-boiled eggs in the middle of the carrots. It looked just like a real bird's nest, except it tasted much better.

1. Preheat the oven to 400°F.

2. Bring a large pot of water to a boil. Fill a large bowl with ice and water and set it nearby. Add the carrots to the boiling water and cook for 5 minutes. Drain the carrots and transfer them to the ice bath to cool. Shred the carrots using a julienne peeler or food processor, and then spread them over a baking sheet. Sprinkle the salt over top.

3. In a small bowl, stir together the melted butter and honey. Pour the honey butter over the carrots and roast for 20 minutes, or until golden brown.

34

TEEN CHEF COOKS

Cilantro–Root Beer Pork Sliders

⚜ SERVES 8
PREP TIME: 10 MIN
COOK TIME: 2 HRS 15 MIN

2 tablespoons olive oil

1 cup chopped yellow onion

3 large garlic cloves, grated

2 tablespoons Latin-style seasoning

8 center-cut pork chops

1 cup root beer

1 teaspoon lime zest

¼ cup fresh lime juice

1 teaspoon finely chopped jalapeño

¼ cup chopped fresh cilantro

½ cup chopped fresh oregano

1 tablespoon smoked paprika

1 teaspoon whole black peppercorns

2 bay leaves

16 slider buns

I love throwing parties, but the problem is that there is always a lot of soda left over afterward. Instead of throwing it away, I use it to make these sliders. If you don't have root beer, you could use cola as a substitute. Once the pork chops are seared and all the ingredients are in the pot, all you have to do is wait for it to be done. The smell coming from your kitchen may be tempting, but trust me, the wait is worth it.

1. In a large pot, heat the oil over medium heat. Add the onion and cook, stirring frequently, for 5 minutes, or until translucent. Stir in the garlic and cook for 30 seconds.

2. Sprinkle 1 tablespoon of the Latin-style seasoning on both sides of the pork chops. Add them to the pot and cook for 4 to 5 minutes on each side, until browned. Add the root beer, making sure the pork chops are not submerged in liquid. Stir in the lime zest, lime juice, jalapeño, cilantro, oregano, paprika, peppercorns, and bay leaves. Cover the pot and reduce the heat to medium-low. Cook for 2 hours, or until the pork chops are tender.

3. Remove the pork chops and slice them into slider-size pieces. Place the sliced pork on the buns and serve immediately.

Warm *Kale* with Apricots, Pecans, and Gorgonzola

⚜ SERVES 4
PREP TIME: 10 MIN
COOK TIME: 10 MIN

1 tablespoon olive oil

¼ cup finely chopped yellow onion

5 cups chopped kale leaves

1 teaspoon minced garlic

½ teaspoon sea salt

¼ teaspoon ground black pepper

¼ cup crumbled Gorgonzola cheese

¼ cup chopped pecans

4 apricots, peeled and chopped into ½-inch chunks (1 cup)

I like to make sure my greens still have bite to them instead of cooking them down too much so they become mushy. Because of the short cook time, the kale remains crunchy. The creamy and salty Gorgonzola goes well with the slightly sweet apricots and nutty pecans. Voilà! It's the perfect combination of flavor, texture, and color.

1. In a large pan, heat the oil over medium heat. Add the onion and cook, stirring frequently, for 3 to 5 minutes, until translucent.

2. Add the kale and cook, stirring occasionally, for 4 minutes, until slightly wilted. Add the garlic, salt, and pepper and cook for 1 minute.

3. Remove from the heat and stir in the cheese, pecans, and apricots.

Stuffed *Onions*

❧ **SERVES 4**
PREP TIME: 15 MIN
COOK TIME: 45 MIN

4 yellow onions, not trimmed or peeled

5 tablespoons olive oil

1 teaspoon minced garlic

1 pound 90% lean ground beef

1 teaspoon sea salt

½ teaspoon ground black pepper

1 tablespoon finely chopped fresh oregano

¼ cup crumbled Gorgonzola cheese

¼ cup pine nuts

¼ cup grated Parmesan cheese

1 cup fresh spinach

The first time I had a stuffed onion, a similar but different take on stuffed bell peppers, was in my culinary arts class. I thought it was brilliant and wondered why I had never thought of making it before. It inspired me to create my own version. I love that the onion is very subtle, sweet, and soft. Pair that with the salty Gorgonzola and crunchy pine nuts, and who can say no?!

1. Preheat the oven to 400°F. Line a baking sheet with aluminum foil.

2. Cut the tops and bottoms off the onions and peel off the skins. Leaving the outer 3 layers intact, make two perpendicular cuts about two-thirds of the way into the center of each onion, without cutting all the way through to the bottom. Scoop out and reserve the inside layers, leaving the 3 outer layers and the bottom third of the onion intact to form a cup. Rub 1 tablespoon of the oil over each hollowed-out onion, coating them inside and out. Place the onions on the prepared baking sheet. Finely chop the reserved onion layers so you have 2 tablespoons (reserve the remainder for another use).

3. In a medium pan, heat the remaining 1 tablespoon oil over medium-high heat. Add the chopped onion and cook, stirring frequently, for 3 to 5 minutes, until translucent. Add the garlic and cook for 30 seconds. Add the beef, salt, and pepper and cook for 10 minutes, or until the beef is browned and fully cooked. Remove from the heat. Stir in the oregano, Gorgonzola, and pine nuts. Evenly distribute the mixture among the onions.

4. Bake for 30 minutes, then remove from the oven and sprinkle 1 tablespoon of the Parmesan on top of each onion. Bake for 5 minutes more, or until Parmesan is melted.

5. Divide the spinach among four plates. Serve one onion on top of each bed of spinach.

Minted Sweet *Peas*

SERVES 6
PREP TIME: 5 MIN
COOK TIME: 35 MIN

1½ cups pearl onions

1 tablespoon olive oil

3½ cups fresh sweet peas

1 tablespoon finely chopped jalapeño (optional)

1½ teaspoons salt

Pinch of ground black pepper

¼ cup chopped fresh mint leaves

Growing up, I was only ever served mushy, bland peas from a can. I thought it was so gross that I swore to never eat peas, until the day I had fresh peas changed my life. I didn't realize how amazing peas could taste! These peas are sweet, so I like to add spice from jalapeño to counter it. If you aren't a fan of a little heat, you can always back off on the amount of jalapeño or just leave it out completely.

1. Bring a medium pot of water to a boil. Fill a large bowl with ice and water and set it nearby. Add the onions to the boiling water and cook for 1 minute. Scoop the onions into the ice bath and let cool, then drain. Peel and halve the onions.

2. In a large pan, heat the oil over medium-high heat. Add the onions and cook, stirring frequently, for 5 minutes, or until browned. Add the peas, jalapeño (if using), salt, and pepper and cook, stirring occasionally, for 5 minutes, or until the peas are fork-tender. Remove from the heat and stir in the mint.

Jerk Shrimp and *Pineapple* Kebabs

⚜ SERVES 4
PREP TIME: 15 MIN
COOK TIME: 5 MIN

2 pounds raw jumbo shrimp, peeled and deveined

½ cup jerk seasoning

1 pineapple, peeled and cut into bite-size chunks

1 lime, cut into 8 wedges

I created this recipe for a birthday party, and it has since become a family favorite. If you are using wooden skewers, make sure to soak them in water for 30 minutes before grilling. This will help prevent them from burning or catching on fire. You can grill the kebabs on an outdoor grill or inside on a stovetop grill pan. Just make sure that if you are cooking them inside, you turn on the exhaust fan above the stove and open a window, because it can get a bit smoky if you don't.

1. Heat a grill to medium-high (400°F) or heat a grill pan over medium-high heat.

2. In a large bowl, combine the shrimp and the jerk seasoning and toss to coat.

3. Thread the shrimp and pineapple onto skewers, alternating them and leaving 1 inch of the skewer exposed on both ends.

4. Grill the skewers for 2½ minutes on each side, or until the shrimp turn pink and are cooked all the way through. Serve immediately with lime wedges.

Roasted *Garlic* Bisque

3 large heads garlic

5 tablespoons olive oil

¾ teaspoon sea salt

¼ teaspoon ground black pepper

2 tablespoons finely chopped
yellow onion

1 tablespoon minced garlic

8 cups vegetable broth

1 tablespoon finely chopped
fresh oregano

1 cup heavy cream

When the garlic is roasted, it releases a delicious sweetness instead of the sharp, intense flavor it would normally have raw. This is a great bisque to make when you are battling a severe cold or feeling even ever so slightly under the weather. Most people think of chicken noodle soup as their go-to sickness cure, but why not switch it up and keep the vampires away at the same time?

1. Preheat the oven to 400°F.

2. Cut the tops off the heads of garlic to expose the cloves, but do not peel them or separate the cloves. Set each head on an individual square of aluminum foil and pour 1 tablespoon of the oil over each. Season each head of garlic with ¼ teaspoon of the salt and a pinch of the pepper, and then tightly wrap the foil around the heads to enclose them. Place the foil-wrapped garlic on a small baking sheet and roast for 30 minutes. Remove from the oven and let the garlic cool.

3. Unwrap the garlic and squeeze the roasted cloves from the skins into a small bowl; discard the skins. Mash the roasted garlic into a paste.

4. In a large pot, heat the remaining 2 tablespoons oil over medium heat. Add the onion and cook, stirring frequently, for 3 to 5 minutes, until translucent. Stir in the minced garlic and roasted garlic paste and cook for 30 seconds. Add the broth, oregano, remaining ½ teaspoon salt, and remaining pepper. Using an immersion blender, purée the mixture directly in the pot until smooth. Increase the heat to high and bring the soup to a boil. Reduce the heat to low, stir in the cream, and simmer for 10 minutes. Serve hot.

Miso-Coconut Beef *Lettuce* Wraps

⚜ SERVES 6
PREP TIME: 10 MIN
COOK TIME: 10 MIN

1 pound flank steak, cut into thin strips against the grain

¼ cup white miso paste

½ cup coconut milk

1 tablespoon toasted sesame oil

1 tablespoon lemongrass paste

2 teaspoons grated fresh ginger

1 tablespoon minced garlic

2 tablespoons sesame seeds

12 romaine lettuce leaves

1 cup shredded carrots

2 tablespoons torn fresh basil

New Orleans has a large Vietnamese population, and there are countless restaurants that serve this cuisine. My favorite Vietnamese restaurant is called Nine Roses. My family has been going there since before I was born. After all these years, we still order the same thing every time we go: make-your-own spring rolls. They bring out a hot portable grill and set it in the center of your table. You use your chopsticks to melt butter on the grill and then lay thin slices of marinated raw beef on top to cook. Once it's cooked, you can start assembling your spring rolls. These lettuce wraps are inspired by those tasty spring rolls that I love so much.

1. Heat a grill to medium-high (400°F) or heat a grill pan over medium-high heat.

2. In a large bowl, mix the beef, miso, coconut milk, oil, lemongrass, ginger, garlic, and sesame seeds.

3. Grill the steak for 5 minutes on each side, or until grill marks appear. Serve the beef in the lettuce leaves, topped with shredded carrots and basil.

Miso-Coconut Beef
Lettuce Wraps
PAGE 45

Mango and Yam Salad

3 yams, peeled and cut into
½-inch cubes

2 mangoes, peeled and chopped

2 tablespoons extra-virgin olive oil

1 tablespoon balsamic vinegar

1 teaspoon fresh lime juice

1 tablespoon F.R.O.G. jam

½ teaspoon sea salt

1 tablespoon chopped fresh mint

F.R.O.G. jam is very common in the south. It is a jam made of Figs, Raspberries, Orange zest, and Ginger. You can usually find it at local farmer's markets, but if you're not able to get your hands on it, you can use fig preserves with ½ teaspoon orange zest and ½ teaspoon grated fresh ginger added.

1. Bring a large pot of water to a boil. Fill a large bowl with ice and water and set it nearby. Add the yams to the boiling water and cook for 10 minutes, or until fork-tender. Scoop the yams into the ice bath and let cool. Drain the yams, transfer them to a medium bowl, and add the mangoes.

2. In a small bowl, whisk together the oil, vinegar, lime juice, jam, and salt. Pour the dressing over the yams and mangoes and mix gently to coat. Serve immediately or refrigerate until ready to serve. Garnish with the mint.

Strawberry-Basil Pavlova

❧ SERVES 8
PREP TIME: 2 HRS
COOK TIME: 1 HR 15 MIN

MERINGUE

4 egg whites

1¼ cups granulated sugar, sifted

2 teaspoons cornstarch, sifted

1 teaspoon distilled white vinegar

1 teaspoon pure vanilla extract

MACERATED STRAWBERRIES

4 cups quartered hulled strawberries

½ cup granulated sugar

¼ cup chopped fresh basil

WHIPPED CREAM

2 cups heavy cream

¼ cup confectioners' sugar

½ teaspoon pure vanilla extract

TO ASSEMBLE

2 tablespoons balsamic vinegar

¼ cup chopped fresh basil

The pavlova is named after the Russian ballerina Anna Pavlova, a particularly light-footed and ethereal dancer. She toured in both New Zealand and Australia, and the two countries have had an ongoing battle as to who invented the sweet treat. Pavlovas are versatile because you can top them with any fruit-and-herb combination. You can also make mini pavlovas by tracing 6-ounce ramekins onto the parchment paper instead of a cake pan.

1. **For the meringue:** Preheat the oven to 350°F. Line a large baking sheet with parchment paper. Using a 9-inch cake pan as a guide, trace a circle onto the parchment paper, and then flip the parchment so the side with the pencil mark is facing the baking sheet.

2. In the bowl of a stand mixer fitted with the whisk attachment, beat the egg whites on medium-high speed until they start to become satiny. With the mixer running, add the granulated sugar 1 tablespoon at a time and whisk until stiff peaks form. Using a spatula, gently fold in the cornstarch, vinegar, and vanilla.

3. Evenly spread the meringue into the circle you traced on the parchment paper. Place in the oven and immediately reduce the oven temperature to 300°F. Bake for 1 hour 15 minutes, then turn off the oven and use the handle of a wooden spoon to prop the door ajar. Allow the meringue to cool in the oven for 1 hour 30 minutes, or until completely cooled.

(RECIPE CONTINUES)

4. **For the macerated strawberries:** While the meringue cools, in a large bowl, stir together the strawberries, granulated sugar, and basil. Cover and refrigerate until ready to assemble the pavlova.

5. **For the whipped cream:** In a large bowl (or in the bowl of a stand mixer fitted with the whisk attachment), whisk together the heavy cream, confectioners' sugar, and vanilla until soft peaks form.

6. To assemble the pavlova, transfer the cooled meringue from the parchment paper to a large plate. Using a wooden spoon, flatten the center of the meringue, leaving a 1-inch border. Evenly spread the whipped cream over the flattened center of the meringue. Using a slotted spoon, scoop the macerated strawberries on top of the whipped cream.

7. Drizzle the balsamic vinegar over the strawberries, sprinkle the basil on top, and serve.

Fruit Crumble

TOPPING

2 cups chopped almonds

1½ cups all-purpose flour

¾ cup packed light brown sugar

5 tablespoons unsalted butter, melted

FILLING

3 tablespoons all-purpose flour

1 cup packed light brown sugar

¼ cup fresh lemon juice

3 cups quartered strawberries

2 peaches, peeled and chopped (1 cup)

4 apricots, peeled and chopped (1 cup)

FOR SERVING

Whipped cream (pages 51 and 52)

This crumble is a great base recipe that allows you to swap in other seasonal fruit in place of the strawberries, peaches, and apricots. For example, you can replace the peaches and apricots with rhubarb to create a strawberry-rhubarb crumble. Or make a more tropical fruit crumble by substituting mango for the strawberries and pineapple for the peaches and apricots. You could also leave it as is and just add thinly shredded fresh mint leaves to complement the fruit. It will turn out delicious any way you decide to make it.

1. Preheat the oven to 350°F.

2. **For the topping:** In a medium bowl, stir together the almonds, flour, brown sugar, and melted butter until thoroughly combined. Set aside.

3. **For the filling:** In a large bowl, stir together the flour, brown sugar, and lemon juice. Gently mix in the strawberries, peaches, and apricots until coated with the flour mixture. Pour the filling into a 9 x 13-inch baking dish and spread it evenly.

4. Sprinkle the topping over the filling and bake for 45 minutes, or until golden brown.

5. Serve topped with a dollop of whipped cream.

Summer

Corn *Guaca*-Salsa

1 cup canned corn kernels, drained

1 tablespoon olive oil

1 avocado, mashed

1 small tomato, chopped

2 teaspoons finely chopped yellow onion

1 garlic clove, minced

1 teaspoon chopped fresh thyme

1 teaspoon chopped fresh parsley

1 teaspoon finely chopped jalapeño

Juice of 1 lime

1 teaspoon sea salt

Tortilla chips, for serving

One day, I was eating guacamole and salsa separately with tortilla chips. I wondered what it would taste like if I mixed them together and put it on a chip. I tried it, and Guaca-Salsa was born. This is now my favorite thing to eat with tortilla chips. If you can't decide on either guacamole or salsa, why not have both?! It's a win-win.

1. Preheat the oven to 400°F. Line a rimmed baking sheet with aluminum foil.

2. Spread the corn over the prepared baking sheet, add the oil, and toss to coat. Roast for 20 minutes. Allow corn to cool for 10 minutes.

3. In a medium bowl, stir together the roasted corn, avocado, tomato, onion, garlic, thyme, parsley, jalapeño, lime juice, and salt. Serve with tortilla chips.

Roasted *Tomatillo* Salsa Verde

❧ SERVES 6
PREP TIME: 5 MIN
COOK TIME: 20 MIN

6 tomatillos

1 cup chopped yellow onion

1 garlic clove, minced

¼ cup fresh cilantro

1 teaspoon fresh lime juice

¼ teaspoon chopped jalapeño

1 teaspoon sea salt

½ teaspoon ground white pepper

1 teaspoon honey

Roasting the tomatillos loosens their skins and makes them easier to peel. It also brings out the natural sweetness of the tomatillos, but they're still very acidic. Adding honey to the salsa verde helps cut that acidity. This recipe makes about 1½ cups of salsa and is delicious with tortilla chips for dipping or as a topping for tacos, my favorite food.

1. Preheat the oven to 400°F. Line a rimmed baking sheet with aluminum foil.

2. Place the tomatillos on the prepared baking sheet. Roast for 20 minutes, or until tomatillos are oozing liquid and the husks begin to pull away from the skin. Remove from the oven and let the tomatillos cool for 10 minutes, then peel them and transfer to a food processor.

3. Add the onion, garlic, cilantro, lime juice, jalapeño, salt, white pepper, and honey to the food processor and blend until smooth.

Pan-Fried *Basil* Tofu

1 tablespoon toasted sesame oil

1 teaspoon lemongrass paste

1 tablespoon soy sauce

1 tablespoon oyster sauce

½ teaspoon finely chopped jalapeño

Handful of fresh basil leaves, torn

1 (16-ounce) package firm tofu, drained and cut into ¼-inch-thick slices

Did you know that tofu is a product of soybeans? It is made from soy milk curds that are pressed into blocks of different textures—soft, firm, and extra-firm. It doesn't have much flavor on its own, but it takes on the flavors of anything you marinate it in. That's what makes it so awesome and versatile!

1. In a large bowl, stir together the oil, lemongrass, soy sauce, oyster sauce, jalapeño, and basil. Add the tofu and turn to coat it with the mixture. Set aside to marinate at room temperature for 15 minutes.

2. In a large skillet, cook the tofu over medium heat for 5 minutes on each side, or until the edges become crisp and the tofu is golden brown.

Veggie Jambalaya

❧ SERVES 6
PREP TIME: 15 MIN
COOK TIME: 40 MIN

2 tablespoons olive oil

½ cup chopped yellow onion

¼ cup chopped bell pepper

¼ cup chopped celery

2 garlic cloves, minced

1 pound vegan andouille sausage, cut into ½-inch-thick rounds

8 ounces chicken seitan, cubed

1 (14.5-ounce) can diced tomatoes

1 tablespoon Creole seasoning

1 cup uncooked long-grain white rice

Chopped scallions, for garnish

When my sister moved away from New Orleans, she still craved our flavorful food. Since she is vegan, she wanted me to create a recipe for a vegan New Orleans jambalaya that she could enjoy and re-create whenever she wanted. I came up with this, and we both love it!

1. In a large pot, heat the oil over medium heat. Add the onion, bell pepper, and celery and cook, stirring frequently, for 3 to 5 minutes, until the onion is translucent. Add the garlic, vegan sausage, and seitan, and cook for 6 to 7 minutes, until the sausage is browned.

2. Stir in the tomatoes, Creole seasoning, rice, and 1 cup water. Cook, stirring occasionally, for 30 minutes, or until the rice has absorbed all the liquid.

3. Garnish with the scallions and serve.

Melon Gazpacho with Oregano Oil

❖ SERVES 4
PREP TIME: 20 MIN
COOK TIME: 0 MIN

GAZPACHO

4 cups chopped ripe seedless watermelon

1 cup chopped cantaloupe

¼ cup balsamic vinegar

¼ cup olive oil

1 teaspoon salt

½ teaspoon ground white pepper

OREGANO OIL

¼ cup extra-virgin olive oil

2 tablespoons fresh oregano

½ teaspoon sea salt

Pinch of ground white pepper

TO ASSEMBLE

4 teaspoons chopped walnuts

4 teaspoons crumbled feta cheese

Gazpacho is a cold soup that originated in Spain. This is a great technique to try with your summer fruit. You could also make a savory version with vegetables. Either way, it's refreshing and tasty.

1. **For the gazpacho:** In a blender, purée the watermelon, cantaloupe, vinegar, olive oil, salt, and white pepper.

2. **For the oregano oil:** In a food processor, combine the oil, oregano, salt, and white pepper and process until the oregano is fully incorporated into the oil.

3. To serve, divide the gazpacho among four bowls, drizzle each with oregano oil, and top evenly with the walnuts and feta.

Potato and *Banana Pepper* Flatbread Pizza

✤ SERVES 2
PREP TIME: 10 MIN
COOK TIME: 35 MIN

Nonstick cooking spray

4 baby Dutch yellow potatoes

1 cup self-rising flour, or
1 cup all-purpose flour mixed with
1¼ teaspoons baking powder, plus
more flour for dusting

1 cup Greek yogurt

2 tablespoons olive oil

2 garlic cloves

1 cup torn fresh mozzarella

½ cup chopped salami

2 large banana peppers, sliced

2 tablespoons chopped fresh basil

Craving pizza, but don't have time to make pizza dough? Well, I have the perfect alternative for you. The dough is super simple because it only uses two ingredients! When I chose the toppings for this dish, I used what was growing in my backyard and what I had available in my house. If you want to use pepperoni instead of salami, go for it. You like tomato sauce on your pizza? Add a layer at the bottom. You can switch the toppings or add whatever you'd like to make your own version.

1. Preheat the oven to 400°F. Line a baking sheet with aluminum foil and coat it with cooking spray.

2. Bring a large pot of water to a boil. Fill a large bowl with ice and water and set it nearby. Add the potatoes to the boiling water and cook for 15 minutes. Drain the potatoes, transfer them to the ice bath, and let cool. Thinly slice the potatoes.

3. In a medium bowl, stir together the flour and yogurt until the mixture forms a ball. Divide the dough in half and place each half on a flour-dusted surface. Roll each half of the dough into a ball, and then roll out the balls to form small rounds (about 10 inches in diameter).

4. Place the dough rounds on the prepared baking sheet. Drizzle 1 tablespoon of the oil on top of each dough round and lightly spread it over the dough with your fingers.

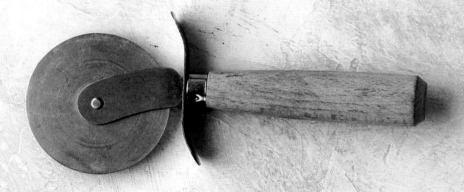

5. Grate 1 garlic clove directly onto each dough round and spread the garlic over the dough with a butter knife. Evenly divide the mozzarella and salami between the pizzas. Arrange the potato slices and banana peppers on top.

6. Bake for 20 minutes, or until the mozzarella is melted and the bottom of the pizza is golden brown. Remove from the oven and let cool slightly.

7. Sprinkle the basil on top and serve.

Potato and Banana Pepper
Flatbread Pizza
PAGES 64 and 65

Oven-Steamed Fresh *Corn*

✦ SERVES 4
PREP TIME: 30 MIN
COOK TIME: 40 MIN

4 ears corn, husks on

This is a foolproof way of roasting corn that my mom taught me many years ago. It works like a charm. Every. Single. Time. You can serve it with a side of compound butter. (But during the summer when the corn is super sweet, I love eating it by itself, without butter. Mmmm!)

1. Preheat the oven to 400°F.

2. Fill the sink or a large bowl with cool water and soak the corn for 30 minutes. Drain the corn, place it on an oven rack, and roast for 40 minutes.

3. Remove the corn from the oven and let cool slightly. When the corn is cool enough to handle, remove and discard the husks and serve.

Fried *Okra*

✤ SERVES 8
PREP TIME: 20 MIN
COOK TIME: 5 MIN

6 cups canola oil, for frying

½ cup buttermilk

1 large egg, beaten

1 cup all-purpose flour

½ cup yellow cornmeal

1 tablespoon Creole seasoning

2 pounds okra, cut into 1-inch pieces

Okra is a vegetable that originated in Africa and came to the United States via the slave trade. It is normally found in gumbo, where it acts as a thickener, but this is my favorite way to eat it. Because the pieces are bite-size, I just can't get enough of them. It makes me want to keep them all for myself!

1. In a large heavy-bottomed pot, heat the oil over high heat.

2. Pour the buttermilk into a small bowl. Put the egg in a second small bowl. In a medium bowl, whisk together the flour, cornmeal, and Creole seasoning.

3. Dip the okra pieces in the buttermilk, then in the egg, letting any excess drip off. Toss the okra in the flour mixture to coat, shaking off any excess.

4. Working in batches, if needed, carefully add the battered okra to the hot oil and fry for 5 minutes, or until golden brown. With a slotted spoon, transfer the fried okra to a paper towel–lined plate to drain. Serve hot.

Sesame *Cucumber* and Cherry Tomato Salad

2 cucumbers, sliced

½ cup cherry tomatoes, halved

1 teaspoon rice wine vinegar

2 teaspoons toasted sesame oil

½ teaspoon sugar

½ teaspoon fish sauce

1 tablespoon sesame seeds

½ teaspoon ground ginger

½ teaspoon sea salt

Everyone loves hosting or attending a summer grill-out, but you always end up eating the same sides. Try switching out a boring salad for this bad boy and watch it disappear from people's plates. It's quick to prepare and refreshing to eat on a hot day.

In a medium bowl, toss together the cucumbers, tomatoes, vinegar, oil, sugar, fish sauce, sesame seeds, ginger, and salt. Cover and refrigerate for 30 minutes. Serve cold.

Vegetable Penne Pasta

❖ SERVES 4
PREP TIME: 15 MIN
COOK TIME: 20 MIN

1 pound whole-wheat penne

2 tablespoons olive oil

1 small yellow onion, finely chopped

2 bell peppers, finely chopped

Kernels from 3 ears corn

1 pound green beans, cut into
2-inch pieces

1 tomato, chopped

1 teaspoon sea salt

¼ teaspoon ground black pepper

2 teaspoons chopped fresh thyme

1 tablespoon chopped fresh basil

1 tablespoon chopped fresh oregano

When I do cooking demonstrations at my local farmer's market, I use in-season ingredients to create a recipe on the spot. I love making pasta dishes because pasta pairs really well with nearly every kind of produce. I remember this demo particularly well because a little boy who was reluctant to eat a pasta dish with so many vegetables decided to try it. When he took a bite, he couldn't get enough of it and came back for seconds and thirds!

1. Bring a large pot of water to a boil. Add the pasta and cook according to the package directions. Drain and set aside.

2. In a large pan, heat the oil over medium heat. Add the onion and bell pepper and cook, stirring frequently, for 5 minutes, or until the onion is translucent. Add the corn and green beans and cook for 5 minutes. Add the tomato, salt, and black pepper.

3. Stir in the pasta, thyme, basil, and oregano and serve immediately.

Eggplant Rollatini

TOMATO SAUCE

1 tablespoon olive oil

¼ cup finely diced yellow onion

½ teaspoon minced garlic

2 (8-ounce) cans tomato sauce

1 (15-ounce) can petite diced tomatoes

1 teaspoon honey

1 teaspoon sea salt

Pinch of ground black pepper

ROLLATINI

2 tablespoons olive oil

1 large eggplant, top cut off, cut lengthwise into ¼-inch-thick slices

1 tablespoon plus 1½ teaspoons sea salt

½ teaspoon plus a pinch ground black pepper

2 tablespoons finely chopped yellow onion

1 teaspoon minced garlic

1½ cups fresh spinach

½ cup ricotta cheese

1 large egg

½ cup shredded Parmesan cheese

½ cup shredded mozzarella cheese

This is a great dish that can be assembled the night before, stored in the fridge, and baked the next day. It also tastes just as good when reheated. Salting the eggplant first is important because it draws out excess water; otherwise, the eggplant will release liquid as it bakes, making your rollatini soggy and watery. Nobody wants that, right? I also like making my own tomato sauce, but using jarred sauce to save time is perfectly acceptable.

1. **For the tomato sauce:** In a medium pot, heat the oil over medium heat. Add the onion and cook, stirring frequently, for 3 to 5 minutes, until translucent. Stir in the garlic and cook for 30 seconds. Stir in the tomato sauce, diced tomatoes, honey, salt, and pepper. Reduce heat to medium-low and simmer for 20 minutes.

2. Preheat the oven to 400°F. Grease an 8-inch square casserole dish with 1 tablespoon of the oil.

3. **For the rollatini:** Meanwhile, put the eggplant slices on a baking sheet and evenly sprinkle them on both sides with 1 tablespoon of the salt. Let sit for 15 minutes to draw out water. Rinse the eggplant slices and pat them dry; rinse and dry the baking sheet and return the eggplant slices to it. Evenly sprinkle both sides of the eggplant slices with 1 teaspoon of the salt and ½ teaspoon of the pepper. Bake for 15 minutes, or until golden brown, flipping the eggplant halfway through. Remove from the oven and let cool for 5 minutes.

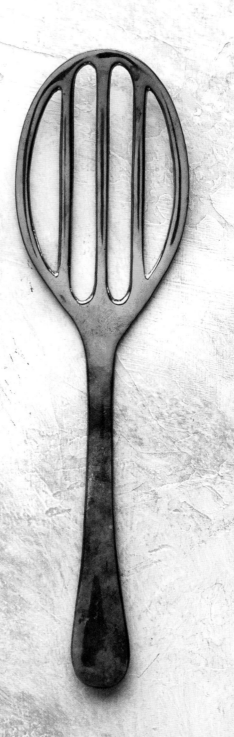

4. In a large pan, heat the remaining 1 tablespoon oil over medium heat. Add the onion and cook, stirring frequently, for 3 to 5 minutes, until translucent. Stir in the garlic and cook for 30 seconds. Add the spinach and cook for 5 minutes, or until wilted. Stir in ¼ teaspoon of salt and the remaining pinch of pepper. Remove from the heat and let cool.

5. In a small bowl, stir together the spinach, ricotta, egg, and remaining ¼ teaspoon salt.

6. Scoop 1 tablespoon of the ricotta mixture onto one end of each eggplant slice. Gently but tightly roll the eggplant around the filling and place the roll seam-side down in the prepared casserole dish. Pour the tomato sauce over the eggplant rolls. Evenly sprinkle the Parmesan and mozzarella over the top. Cover the dish with aluminum foil and bake for 20 minutes, then remove the foil and bake for 10 minutes more, or until the cheese is golden brown. Remove from the oven and let sit for 10 minutes before serving.

Grilled *Squash* and Tomato Salad

3 yellow squash, sliced ¼-inch-thick lengthwise

1 tablespoon olive oil

1 teaspoon sea salt

1 large tomato, chopped

1 teaspoon Italian seasoning

1 cup torn fresh basil leaves

1 teaspoon chopped fresh oregano

1 teaspoon chopped fresh parsley

1 teaspoon chopped fresh garlic chives or chives

By itself, yellow squash does not have much flavor. Grilling it adds beautiful char marks and that yummy grilled flavor everyone loves. The squash works so well with fresh tomato and herbs. This is a great side to serve at summer picnics.

1. Heat a grill pan over high heat.

2. Coat the squash on both sides with the oil and sprinkle both sides with ½ teaspoon of the salt. Grill the squash for 2½ minutes on each side, or until char marks develop.

3. Transfer the squash slices to a cutting board and dice them into small pieces. Place in a large bowl and add the tomato, Italian seasoning, basil, oregano, parsley, garlic chives, and remaining ½ teaspoon salt. Toss and serve.

Tomato Basil Bisque

2 tablespoons olive oil

1 yellow onion, chopped

4 garlic cloves, minced

3 medium tomatoes, chopped

1 (14.5-ounce) can diced tomatoes

1 cup chopped fresh basil

1 tablespoon chopped fresh oregano

1 tablespoon chopped fresh thyme

4 cups chicken broth

½ cup shredded Parmesan cheese

½ cup heavy cream

1 teaspoon sea salt

A bisque is a smooth, thick soup that is usually puréed. This is a classic bisque that you can't go wrong with. I usually serve my tomato basil bisque with French bread, while other people love to serve it with a grilled cheese sandwich. Either tastes delicious when dipped in the bisque.

1. In a large pot, heat the oil over medium heat. Add the onion and cook, stirring frequently, for 5 minutes, or until translucent. Stir in the garlic and cook for 30 seconds. Add the fresh tomatoes, diced tomatoes, basil, oregano, and thyme. Cook for 5 to 7 minutes, until the tomatoes begin to break down. Add the broth.

2. Using an immersion blender, purée the soup directly in the pot until smooth. Stir in the cheese, heavy cream, and salt.

3. Reduce the heat to low and simmer for 30 minutes before serving.

Zucchini Parmesan Fries

SERVES 4
PREP TIME: 10 MIN
COOK TIME: 30 MIN

Olive oil cooking spray

2 large eggs

½ cup Italian-style bread crumbs

½ cup panko bread crumbs

½ cup grated Parmesan cheese

6 small zucchini, tops cut off and quartered lengthwise

Like the avocado fries on page 27, these zucchini fries are a healthier alternative to french fries. Try them alongside your favorite burger to spruce up your meal. You can also serve them with marinara for dipping. You can use store-bought marinara or make your own while the zucchini fries are baking.

1. Preheat the oven to 400°F. Line a baking sheet with aluminum foil and coat with cooking spray.

2. Put the eggs in a shallow bowl and beat them lightly. In a separate shallow bowl, combine the Italian-style bread crumbs, panko, and cheese.

3. Dip the zucchini pieces in the egg to coat, letting any excess drip off, then coat them with the bread crumb mixture. Arrange the zucchini pieces on the prepared baking sheet and spritz them with cooking spray. Bake for 30 minutes, or until fork-tender and golden brown.

Watermelon
Feta Panzanella

⚜ SERVES 8
PREP TIME: 15 MIN
COOK TIME: 3 MIN

1 baguette, cut into 1-inch cubes

4 tablespoons olive oil

5 cups watermelon chunks

3 peaches, pitted and cut into chunks

6 tomatoes, chopped

½ cup crumbled feta cheese

¼ cup balsamic vinegar

2 tablespoons honey

Panzanella is a Tuscan bread salad that is traditionally made with chunks of stale bread, softened by soaking in a vinaigrette, with tomatoes and other fresh vegetables. This is another recipe that I created for a cooking demonstration at my local farmer's market. I re-created this dish at home and toasted the bread in the broiler for a faster cooking time. I could eat this one for a week straight and not get tired of it! That's how amazing it is.

1. Preheat the broiler.

2. Place the baguette cubes on a baking sheet and drizzle them with 1 tablespoon of the oil. Broil for 3 minutes, or until golden brown.

3. In a large bowl, toss together the toasted bread cubes, watermelon, peach, tomato, and feta.

4. In a small jar with a lid, combine the vinegar, remaining 3 tablespoons oil, and honey. Cover and shake until emulsified.

5. Pour the vinaigrette over the bread and toss to combine. The bread should soften as it soaks up some of the vinaigrette and the juices from the fruit.

Nectarine, Peach, and Spearmint Salad

2 nectarines, pitted and sliced

2 peaches, pitted and sliced

¼ cup unsweetened dried cranberries

¼ cup golden raisins

2 tablespoons chopped fresh spearmint

1 tablespoon honey, warmed

This salad is a perfect party dish. When most people think of salad, they think of greens with vegetables and a dressing. But a salad can also be sweet and made with fruit. Pairing fruit with herbs is one of my favorite go-tos. They always work well together.

In a medium bowl, toss together the nectarines, peaches, cranberries, raisins, spearmint, and honey. Cover and refrigerate for 30 minutes. Serve cold.

Warm *Peach* and Tomato Bruschetta

4 tablespoons olive oil

1 baguette, cut into ½-inch-thick slices

3 tomatoes, chopped

2 peaches, pitted and chopped

½ cup crumbled feta cheese

½ teaspoon sea salt

¼ teaspoon ground black pepper

2 tablespoons balsamic vinegar

1 tablespoon peach jam

This is another recipe I created for a cooking demonstration at my local farmer's market. After pasta dishes, bruschetta is my other go-to, because you can pair just about any fruits or vegetables and pile them on top of crostini. Peaches and tomatoes might be one of my favorite combinations ever. The sweet peaches go so well with the acidic tomatoes, and the vinaigrette brings everything together.

1. Heat a large skillet over medium heat. Evenly drizzle both sides of the baguette slices with 2 tablespoons of the oil. Place the bread in the pan and toast for 3 to 5 minutes, or until lightly browned on both sides, about 3 to 5 minutes. Remove the slices from the pan and set them aside on a large plate or platter.

2. In the same pan, combine the tomatoes, peaches, feta, salt, and pepper and cook, stirring frequently, for 5 minutes, or until the tomatoes start to break down. Turn off the heat. Spoon the warm tomato-peach mixture onto the baguette slices.

3. In a small jar with a lid, combine the remaining 2 tablespoons oil, vinegar, and jam. Cover and shake until emulsified.

4. Drizzle the vinaigrette on top of the bruschetta and serve.

Blueberry Slump

⚜ **SERVES 5**
PREP TIME: 10 MIN
COOK TIME: 30 MIN

1 cup all-purpose flour

½ cup plus 1 tablespoon sugar

1 teaspoon baking powder

¼ teaspoon sea salt

2 tablespoons unsalted butter, cubed and chilled

½ cup whole milk

2 cups blueberries

2 tablespoons fresh lemon juice

5 scoops of vanilla ice cream, for serving

A slump is a classic New England dessert with a base of fruit on the bottom and biscuit dough baked on top. Chef Frank Brigtsen introduced me to blueberry slump when we made Paul Prudhomme's recipe together in my culinary arts class. I was inspired to make my own version.

1. Preheat the oven to 400°F.

2. In a medium bowl, whisk together the flour, ½ cup of the sugar, baking powder, and salt. Mix the butter into the flour mixture with your hands until the butter is in pea-size pieces. Stir in the milk and set the batter aside.

3. In a large cast-iron skillet, combine the blueberries, lemon juice, and remaining 1 tablespoon sugar and cook over medium heat for 5 minutes, or until blueberries have reduced and begun to create a liquid.

4. Drop ¼-cup scoops of the biscuit batter over the blueberries. Transfer the skillet to the oven and bake for 25 minutes, or until the biscuits are cooked through. Wearing oven mitts, carefully remove the skillet from the oven. Let cool for 5 minutes before serving.

5. Serve each biscuit and blueberries with a scoop of vanilla ice cream.

Mini *Blackberry* Cobbler

❖ SERVES 8
PREP TIME: 10 MIN
COOK TIME: 30 MIN

1½ cups fresh blackberries

1 tablespoon fresh lemon juice

2 cups self-rising flour, or
2 cups all-purpose flour mixed with
2½ teaspoons baking powder

1 cup plus 1 tablespoon sugar

½ cup (1 stick) unsalted butter,
melted

1 large egg

If I can put something in a ramekin, I will. By baking this cobbler in individual ramekins, you don't have to worry about cutting it evenly and trying to serve everyone the same amount. This makes it super easy to serve to a group, especially if you love to entertain.

1. Preheat the oven to 350°F.

2. In a small bowl, toss the blackberries in the lemon juice. Divide the blackberries evenly among eight 6-ounce ramekins.

3. In a medium bowl, whisk together the flour, 1 cup of the sugar, melted butter, and egg until the mixture comes together in large crumbs. Evenly fill each ramekin with the crumble. Evenly sprinkle the remaining 1 tablespoon sugar over the crumble topping in each ramekin.

4. Bake for 25 to 30 minutes, until the crumble is golden brown and the blackberry juices are oozing through the crumble.

Cherry Clafoutis

3 tablespoons unsalted butter, melted

½ cup all-purpose flour, sifted

½ cup sugar, sifted

3 large eggs

1 teaspoon pure almond extract

1 cup whole milk

3 cups cherries, pitted

This is a classic French dessert similar to a Dutch baby. It's very simple to make because all you have to do is stir together the ingredients and dump the batter into a pan. Once it's been baked, it becomes custardlike. You can also exchange the cherries for any other seasonal berries or a combination of chopped in-season fruits.

1. Preheat the oven to 325°F. Coat a cast-iron skillet with 1 tablespoon of the melted butter.

2. Put the flour in a large bowl and set aside.

3. In a medium bowl, whisk together the sugar and remaining 2 tablespoons melted butter. Beat in the eggs one at a time. Whisk in the almond extract and milk. While whisking, gradually add the egg mixture to the flour and whisk until combined.

4. Pour the batter into the prepared skillet. Evenly distribute the cherries on top of the batter. Bake for 40 minutes, or until cooked through and golden brown. Wearing oven mitts, carefully remove the skillet from the oven. Let cool for 5 minutes before serving.

Fall

Cheesy *Broccoli* and Potato Soup

❧ SERVES 4
PREP TIME: 15 MIN
COOK TIME: 35 MIN

1 head broccoli, cut into bite-size pieces

1 tablespoon olive oil

1 cup chopped yellow onion

2 garlic cloves, minced

6 cups vegetable broth

2 pounds potatoes, peeled and cut into chunks

2 cups shredded cheddar cheese

1 teaspoon sea salt

¼ teaspoon ground black pepper

Cheese and broccoli—such a fabulous combination. I especially love it in the form of this classic soup. By puréeing the cooked potatoes with the vegetable broth, they act as a thickener for the soup. A thick soup is great for serving in individual bread bowls—it's a great comfort meal all in one.

1. Bring a large pot of water to a boil. Fill a large bowl with ice and water and set it nearby. Add the broccoli to the boiling water and cook for 2 minutes. Drain the broccoli and transfer it to the ice bath; let cool, about 1 minute, then drain.

2. In a large pot, heat the oil over medium heat. Add the onion and cook, stirring frequently, for 3 to 5 minutes, until translucent. Stir in the garlic and cook for 30 seconds. Increase the heat to medium-high and add the broth and potatoes. Cook, stirring occasionally, for 15 to 20 minutes, until the potatoes begin to fall apart.

3. Using an immersion blender, blend the mixture directly in the pot until smooth. Reduce the heat to medium, add the cheese, and stir until it has melted. Add the broccoli, salt, and pepper and cook for 10 minutes more, or until the broccoli is tender to your liking.

Italian Sausage Stuffed *Bell Peppers*

✤ SERVES 4
PREP TIME: 15 MIN
COOK TIME: 50 MIN

1 tablespoon olive oil

1 cup chopped yellow onion

3 cups sliced mushrooms

2 garlic cloves, minced

1 tablespoon chopped fresh parsley

1 pound Italian sausages

1 tablespoon Creole seasoning

1 teaspoon sea salt

2 cups Italian-style bread crumbs

½ cup whole milk

4 bell peppers, tops cut off and cored

4 tablespoons shredded mozzarella cheese

When choosing what color bell peppers to use, think about the flavor of each color. It sounds funny to say that different-colored peppers have different flavors, but it's true. Green bell peppers are more pungent, while yellow and orange bell peppers are sweeter. Red bell peppers are the sweetest because they have matured the longest. I tend to use a variety and then let my guests choose which ones they want. I love using bell peppers as a bowl because you can stuff them with practically any filling and create a fantastic meal.

1. Preheat the oven to 375°F.

2. In a large pan, heat the oil over medium heat. Add the onion, mushrooms, garlic, and parsley and cook, stirring frequently, for 5 to 7 minutes, until the onion is translucent. Squeeze the sausages out of their casings into the pan and cook, breaking up the sausage with a wooden spoon as it cooks, for 8 to 10 minutes, until browned. Stir in the Creole seasoning, salt, bread crumbs, and milk. Remove from the heat.

3. Stand the bell peppers upright in an 8-inch casserole dish. Evenly distribute the stuffing among the peppers. Sprinkle 1 tablespoon of the cheese on each pepper. Bake for 30 minutes, or until the peppers are fork-tender and the cheese is melted. Serve immediately.

Raw Brussels
Sprout Salad
PAGE 98

Raw *Brussels Sprout* Salad

⚜ SERVES 8
PREP TIME: 15 MIN
COOK TIME: 0 MIN

1 pound Brussels sprouts, thinly sliced

1 cup thinly sliced strawberries

2 satsumas, peeled, segmented, and each segment cut in half

¼ cup pine nuts

¼ cup grated Asiago cheese

½ cup fresh satsuma juice

¼ cup blood orange syrup

¼ cup olive oil

Pinch of sea salt

This is a different way to prepare Brussels sprouts. I love the crunch that the raw sprouts add to the salad. Plus, the fruit adds a bit of sweetness to counteract the sprouts' slight bite. If you can't get your hands on satsumas, you can always use mandarin oranges instead. The blood orange syrup can be found at your local farmer's market.

1. In a large bowl, toss together the Brussels sprouts, strawberries, satsumas, pine nuts, and cheese until combined.

2. In a small jar with a lid, combine the satsuma juice, blood orange syrup, oil, and salt. Cover the jar and shake until emulsified.

3. Pour the vinaigrette over the salad and mix thoroughly.

Pan-Fried Pork Chops with Warm Apple-*Carrot* Slaw

⚜ SERVES 6
PREP TIME: 20 MIN
COOK TIME: 20 MIN

2 tablespoons Creole seasoning

6 (4-ounce) boneless pork chops, ½ inch thick each

2 tablespoons olive oil

½ cup cider vinegar

½ cup packed light brown sugar

½ cup thinly sliced yellow onion

3 apples, peeled and sliced (3 cups)

5 medium carrots, cut into matchsticks (2 cups)

¼ cup unsweetened dried cranberries

Chopped fresh sage, for garnish

I created this recipe for a cooking demonstration at an international produce conference. I had to develop a dish using seasonal produce. Apples were in-season at the time, and I figured that they go well with pork. The two ingredients are like best friends: once you put them together, they are inseparable. I came up with this recipe and fell in love with the slaw-and-pork-chop combination.

1. Rub the Creole seasoning on both sides of the pork chops.

2. In a large pan, heat the oil over medium heat. Add the pork chops and cook for 3 to 4 minutes on each side, until golden brown. Transfer the pork chops to a large plate or platter and cover to keep warm.

3. Add the vinegar to the pan and stir, scraping up any browned bits from the bottom. Add the brown sugar and stir until incorporated. Add the onion and cook, stirring frequently, for 3 to 5 minutes, until translucent. Add the apples and carrots and cook for 5 to 7 minutes, until the apples begin to soften. Stir in the cranberries and pour the mixture over the warm pork chops.

4. Garnish with sage and serve immediately.

Lemon-Garlic
Cauliflower Steaks

½ cup olive oil

2 tablespoons fresh lemon juice

3 garlic cloves, minced

1 teaspoon sea salt

½ teaspoon ground black pepper

1 head cauliflower, leaves removed, cut through the core into 1-inch-thick steaks

This is a quick meal that's easy to throw together. It does not take as much work since the cauliflower is cut into thick steaks. It's perfect if you are having a steak night but some of your guests are vegetarian or vegan, or if you just want to cook a healthier option for dinner.

1. Preheat the oven to 400°F. Line a baking sheet with aluminum foil.

2. In a medium bowl, whisk together the oil, lemon juice, garlic, salt, and pepper. Coat the cauliflower steaks with the oil mixture and place them on the prepared baking sheet. Roast for 35 to 40 minutes, until the cauliflower is tender and golden brown, flipping the steaks halfway through to ensure both sides brown evenly.

Roasted *Cauliflower* Fried Rice

⚜ SERVES 12
PREP TIME: 15 MIN
COOK TIME: 35 MIN

1 head cauliflower, cut into small florets

2 tablespoons olive oil, plus more as needed

½ teaspoon sea salt

3 cups uncooked rice

6 large eggs, beaten

5 slices bacon, chopped

5 garlic cloves, minced

2 large smoked sausage links, chopped

4 scallions, chopped

¼ cup soy sauce

Because this makes a jumbo batch of fried rice, it's a wonderful dish to serve at a party or a large family gathering. I made this fried rice for my own birthday party, and all my guests loved it. By the end of the night, the fried rice was demolished, and I had no leftovers for lunch the next day. At least that was a sign that it was tasty!

1. Preheat the oven to 400°F. Line a baking sheet with aluminum foil.

2. Place the cauliflower on the prepared baking sheet. Drizzle with the oil and sprinkle with the salt. Roast for 20 minutes, or until fork-tender and golden brown.

3. In a large pot, combine the rice and 5 cups water and bring to a boil over high heat. Reduce the heat to medium, cover, and simmer, stirring occasionally, for 17 minutes, or until the rice absorbs all the liquid.

4. Coat the bottom of a medium pan with oil and heat it over medium-low heat. Add the eggs and cook, stirring occasionally, for 5 minutes, or until the eggs are scrambled and fluffy.

5. In a wok, cook the bacon over medium-high heat for 5 minutes, or until crispy. Add the garlic and smoked sausage. Cook for 7 to 8 minutes, until the sausage begins to brown and get crispy. Stir in the roasted cauliflower, scallions, and cooked rice. Add the soy sauce and stir until it is fully incorporated and the rice is tinted brown. Fold in the scrambled eggs. Serve warm.

Roasted *Corn* and Forbidden Rice Salad

SERVES 4
PREP TIME: 45 MIN
COOK TIME: 45 MIN

Kernels from 4 ears corn

2 tablespoons olive oil

1 cup uncooked black rice, rinsed

2 tablespoons chopped fresh mint

1 tablespoon sesame seeds

½ teaspoon ground ginger

1 teaspoon sea salt

1 teaspoon fresh lemon juice

1 teaspoon toasted sesame oil

Black rice is often called Forbidden rice because long ago, Chinese emperors would not allow the general population to eat the rare grain. Back then it was reserved for royalty, but now it's available to everyone. Black rice is unmilled and still has its husk intact, which gives it its deep, dark color. Because it still has its husk, it takes about the same amount of time to cook as brown rice does. Be forewarned: It may stain your fingers once cooked.

1. Preheat the oven to 400°F. Line a baking sheet with aluminum foil.

2. Place the corn kernels on the prepared baking sheet and coat with the olive oil. Roast for 20 minutes, or until golden brown.

3. In a medium pot, combine the rice and 1¾ cups water. Bring to a boil over high heat. Reduce the heat to medium, cover, and simmer for 45 minutes, or until the rice absorbs all the liquid.

4. In a large bowl, stir together the roasted corn, cooked rice, mint, sesame seeds, ginger, salt, lemon juice, and sesame oil. Refrigerate for 30 minutes, or until cold, before serving.

Chicken Piccata

⚜ SERVES 6
PREP TIME: 15 MIN
COOK TIME: 20 MIN

1 pound whole-wheat linguine

1 cup all-purpose flour

1 tablespoon Italian seasoning

2 teaspoons sea salt

½ teaspoon ground black pepper

½ cup whole milk

3 boneless, skinless chicken breasts, each cut into 2 thin cutlets

6 tablespoons olive oil

⅔ cup chicken broth

1 cup fresh lemon juice

1 tablespoon capers

1 lemon, cut into 6 wedges

Winner, winner, chicken dinner! I'm always ready for a scrumptious, lemony Italian chicken. If you're in a rut and can't think of what to cook, this is a great dish for you to make. This recipe calls for ingredients that most people already have on hand, so you don't even have to worry about making a trip the store.

1. Bring a large pot of water to a boil. Add the pasta and cook according to the package directions. Drain and set aside.

2. In a medium bowl, whisk together the flour, Italian seasoning, 1 teaspoon of the salt, and the pepper. Put the milk in a separate medium bowl. Dip the chicken pieces in the milk, letting any excess drip off, then dredge them in the seasoned flour to coat.

3. Use two large skillets to cook all the chicken at once without crowding the pans. In each pan, heat 3 tablespoons of the oil over medium-high heat. Divide the chicken pieces between the pans and cook for 7 to 8 minutes on each side, until crisp and golden brown.

4. Add ⅓ cup of the broth and ½ cup of the lemon juice to each pan. Reduce the heat to medium and simmer for 3 to 4 minutes. Stir half the capers and ½ teaspoon of the salt into each pan.

5. Serve the chicken over the pasta with a wedge of lemon for squeezing.

Orange-Ginger Tuna *Lettuce* Wraps

SERVES 6
PREP TIME: 1 HR 15 MIN
COOK TIME: 10 MIN

TUNA

1 teaspoon orange zest

½ cup fresh orange juice

¼ cup soy sauce

1 tablespoon grated fresh ginger

½ teaspoon minced garlic

2 teaspoons honey

¼ cup packed light brown sugar

1 teaspoon sesame seeds

¼ teaspoon sea salt

1½ pounds tuna, skin removed, cut into 1-inch-thick steaks

SAUCE

¼ cup soy sauce

2 tablespoons toasted sesame oil

4 teaspoons grated fresh ginger

2 teaspoons minced garlic

TO ASSEMBLE

12 romaine lettuce leaves

1 cup grated carrot

These lettuce wraps are a healthier option than eating the tuna on bread as a sandwich. When you bite into the lettuce wrap, you immediately encounter the slightly spicy ginger, which pairs very well with the sweet orange that you taste after you swallow it. That little drizzle of sauce brings everything together.

1. **For the tuna:** In a large bowl, stir together the orange zest, orange juice, soy sauce, ginger, garlic, honey, sugar, sesame seeds, and salt. Add the tuna, tossing to coat it in the sauce, and set aside to marinate in the refrigerator for 1 hour.

2. Heat a large pan over medium-high heat. Add the tuna and sear on each side for 2½ minutes. Transfer the tuna to a cutting board and allow to rest for 5 minutes.

3. **For the sauce:** In a small bowl, mix together the soy sauce, oil, ginger, and garlic.

4. To assemble the wraps, slice the tuna into ½-inch chunks. Place 2 lettuce leaves on each plate. Scoop ¼ cup of the tuna onto each leaf. Sprinkle 1 tablespoon of the carrot on top of each tuna wrap and drizzle with 1 teaspoon of the sauce.

Slow Cooker
Mango-Pepper Pork

⚜ SERVES 6

PREP TIME: 10 MIN

COOK TIME: 8 HRS

4 cups chicken broth

2 small yellow onions, sliced

5 garlic cloves

1 tablespoon Latin-style seasoning

1 tablespoon paprika

½ teaspoon ground cumin

2 mangoes, chopped

5 chiles de árbol

1 (3-pound) pork tenderloin

Cooked rice, for serving

Sometimes it's nice to whip out the slow cooker and let your pots and pans have a spa day. The slow cooker does the hard part for you. You can prep all the ingredients the night before and put them in the slow cooker in the morning. When you come home from a busy day, dinner is ready and waiting for you!

1. In a slow cooker, stir together the broth, onions, garlic, Latin-style seasoning, paprika, cumin, mangoes, and chiles. Add the pork tenderloin. Cover and cook on low for 8 hours.

2. Using tongs, transfer the pork to a platter and serve it with rice and the juice from the slow cooker.

Onion, Bacon, and Jalapeño Marmalade

⚜ SERVES 16
PREP TIME: 15 MIN
COOK TIME: 1 HR 50 MIN

2 pounds sliced bacon

2½ pounds cipollini onions (about 40 onions), sliced

1 tablespoon finely chopped jalapeño

¼ cup cider vinegar

½ cup root beer

½ cup packed light brown sugar

1 teaspoon sea salt

Crostini, for serving

In my culinary arts class, we made a bacon onion jam to sell in our holiday marketplace. It's so good that it inspired me to make something similar at home. It's not your traditional sweet fruit marmalade, but rather a savory one. The smokiness from the bacon pairs well with the sweetness of the onion and root beer. The jalapeño adds a touch of heat. Get in mah belly! This can also be used as a spread on a sandwich or toast or served over softened cream cheese with crackers for spreading.

1. In a large pan, cook the bacon for 3 to 5 minutes, until crispy, flipping the slices halfway through. Transfer the bacon to a paper towel–lined plate to drain and cool slightly. Spoon 2 tablespoons of the rendered bacon fat into a large Dutch oven and discard the rest (or reserve it for another use).

2. Heat the bacon fat over medium heat. Add the onions and cook, stirring frequently, for 5 to 7 minutes, until translucent. Crumble the bacon into the pot and add the jalapeño, vinegar, ¼ cup of the root beer, brown sugar, and salt. Reduce the heat to medium-low and simmer, stirring occasionally, for 1 hour 30 minutes, until the liquid begins to evaporate. Add the remaining ¼ cup root beer and cook for 10 minutes more, or until the onions are brown and soft and the liquid has nearly evaporated.

3. Serve on top of crostini.

Mushroom and Cream Cheese Wontons

1 tablespoon toasted sesame oil

3 cups finely chopped portobello mushrooms

2 tablespoons finely chopped shallot

1 teaspoon minced garlic

½ teaspoon Chinese five-spice powder

½ teaspoon sea salt

¼ teaspoon ground white pepper

1 (8-ounce) package cream cheese

1 (12-ounce) package wonton wrappers

1 large egg, beaten

2 cups vegetable oil, for frying

This is a great party hors d'oeuvre to pass on a tray or serve as a side with a meal. Either way, it's sure to hit the spot. If you have leftovers and want to reheat them, place them on a wire rack set on a rimmed baking sheet and heat them in a preheated 350°F oven for 5 minutes. The wire rack allows air to circulate around them, keeping their crispiness intact.

1. In a medium pan, heat the sesame oil over medium-low heat. Add the mushrooms, shallot, garlic, five-spice powder, salt, and pepper and cook for 5 to 7 minutes, until the mushrooms are soft.

2. Transfer the mushroom mixture to a large bowl and add the cream cheese. Stir to combine.

3. Spoon 1 tablespoon of the mushroom filling into the center of a wonton wrapper. Put the egg in a small bowl. Dip a finger in the egg and run it over the edges of the wonton wrapper. Fold the wrapper in half and seal the edges. Set the finished wonton on a large plate and repeat until you run out of the filling.

4. In a large pot, heat the vegetable oil over medium-high heat. Working in batches as needed, add the wontons and fry for 2 to 3 minutes on each side, until golden brown. Transfer the fried wontons to a paper towel–lined plate to drain. Serve hot.

Oregano Brown Butter
Potatoes

⚜ SERVES 4
PREP TIME: 5 MIN
COOK TIME: 30 MIN

8 baby Dutch yellow potatoes, quartered

3 tablespoons unsalted butter

2 tablespoons chopped fresh oregano

1 teaspoon sea salt

½ teaspoon ground black pepper

Brown butter can make anything taste ten times better. It adds richness, depth of flavor, and a beautiful color. Just be sure to watch the butter carefully as it cooks so it doesn't burn. The oregano is wonderful with the brown butter because of its slightly peppery and strong taste.

1. Bring a large pot of water to a boil. Add the potatoes and cook for 15 to 20 minutes, until fork-tender. Drain and set aside.

2. In a medium pan, melt the butter over medium heat. Cook the melted butter, stirring occasionally, for 2 to 3 minutes, until it begins to brown. Add the oregano and cook, stirring, for 30 seconds. Add the potatoes, salt, and pepper. Cook for 7 to 8 minutes, until the potatoes begin to brown and develop crispy edges.

Spinach and Mushroom Quiche

Nonstick cooking spray

1 tablespoon olive oil

1 cup sliced baby portobello mushrooms

¼ teaspoon sea salt

10 large eggs

½ cup heavy cream

½ cup whole milk

1 tablespoon Creole seasoning

2 sheets frozen puff pastry, thawed

3 cups baby spinach

1 cup crumbled feta cheese

Quiche is one of my household breakfast staples. I love it because it can be assembled the night before and popped into the oven the next morning. You could even bake it ahead of time, freeze it, and reheat it in the oven whenever you're ready to eat it. Quiches are like savory tarts, so they are usually made with a pie crust. To make the process a little easier, I like to use prepared puff pastry for the crust.

1. Preheat the oven to 400°F. Grease a 9 x 13-inch baking dish with cooking spray.

2. Lightly coat the bottom of a medium pan with oil and heat over medium heat. Add the mushrooms and cook for 3 to 5 minutes, until softened. Stir in the salt, remove from the heat, and set aside.

3. In a large bowl, whisk together the eggs, cream, milk, and Creole seasoning. Set aside.

4. Line the prepared baking dish with the puff pastry sheets, cutting them to fit, if necessary. Evenly distribute the mushrooms over the puff pastry. Spread the spinach evenly over the mushrooms and sprinkle evenly with the feta. Pour the egg mixture into the baking dish.

5. Bake for 30 minutes, or until cooked through and golden brown. Remove from the oven and allow to cool for 10 minutes before serving.

Spinach and
Mushroom Quiche
PAGE 113

Zucchini and Shiitake Spaghetti

✦ SERVES 8
PREP TIME: 15 MIN
COOK TIME: 30 MIN

2 pounds whole-wheat spaghetti

2 tablespoons olive oil

½ cup chopped yellow onion

1 garlic clove, minced

½ pound fresh field peas, snapped into 2-inch pieces (2 cups)

2 cups chopped shiitake mushrooms

2 large zucchini, tops cut off and sliced into 3- to 4-inch-long ribbons

1 tablespoon Creole seasoning

1 teaspoon sea salt

1 large tomato, chopped

1 cup crumbled goat cheese

2 tablespoons fresh lemon juice

The goat cheese and lemon juice really add dimension to this pasta dish. And all the veggies in it make it healthy. In this recipe, I use field peas, which are very common in the South but may not be readily available in other places. If you can't find field peas, you can use snap peas instead. They will have the same crunchiness as field peas. If you are using snap peas, you do not have to break them in half.

1. Bring a large pot of water to a boil. Add the pasta and cook according to the package directions. Drain and set aside.

2. In a large pan, heat the oil over medium heat. Add the onion and cook, stirring frequently, for 3 to 5 minutes, until translucent. Stir in the garlic and cook for 30 seconds. Add the peas and cook, stirring frequently, for 5 minutes. Add the mushrooms and cook for 2 minutes. Add the zucchini ribbons, Creole seasoning, and salt and stir to combine. Cook for 3 minutes, then add the tomatoes and cook for 1 minute more.

3. Add the cooked pasta, goat cheese, and lemon juice and toss to combine. Serve immediately.

Ginger-*Yam* Hash

3 yams, peeled and grated on the large holes of a box grater

¼ cup chopped bacon

¼ cup finely chopped shallot

1 teaspoon minced garlic

1 teaspoon grated fresh ginger

1 teaspoon sea salt

Instead of making a traditional hash using white potatoes, I've switched things up by using yams. Ginger and yam is a delectable pairing. The crispy bacon adds saltiness and texture. This is perfect for breakfast or as a side dish for lunch or dinner. To take it one step further, you can create wells in the hash and crack eggs into them. Cover the pan with a lid and cook until the whites are set. That way, you can have a bite of the hash with eggs, and you don't even have to dirty another pan.

1. Put the yams in a double layer of cheesecloth, bring the edges together, and twist to squeeze out moisture from the yams; set them aside.

2. In a large pan, cook the bacon over medium heat for 3 to 5 minutes, until crispy. Add the shallot and cook, stirring frequently, for 3 to 5 minutes, until translucent. Stir in the garlic and ginger and cook for 30 seconds. Add the yams and salt and stir to combine. Cook for 5 minutes without moving the yams, or until the bottom is browned (check this by lifting the edge of the hash with a spatula). Stir and cook for 5 minutes more, or until fork-tender.

Sesame-*Ginger* Egg Salad

12 large eggs

½ cup mayonnaise

2 tablespoons Creole mustard

1 teaspoon toasted sesame oil

2 tablespoons sesame seeds

1 teaspoon grated fresh ginger

2 tablespoons chopped fresh mint

1 teaspoon sea salt

½ teaspoon ground black pepper

Crackers or sandwich bread, for serving

I learned this method of hard-boiling eggs in my culinary arts class. We call it the 5-Minute Method. It is foolproof and cooks the eggs perfectly every time. This egg salad is a fresh new take on traditional egg salad. I could eat the entire bowl myself, but I guess it's nice to share every once in a while . . .

1. Fill a large bowl with ice and water and set it nearby. Place the eggs in a large pot and add cold water to cover. Bring the water to a boil. Cook the eggs for 5 minutes, then turn off the heat and let the eggs sit in the hot water for 5 minutes more. Transfer the eggs to the ice bath and let cool for 5 minutes.

2. Peel the eggs and chop them into small pieces. Transfer the eggs to a large bowl and add the mayonnaise, mustard, oil, sesame seeds, ginger, mint, salt, and pepper. Stir to combine.

3. Serve with crackers for dipping or on bread as a sandwich.

Cranberry-Apple Compote

❧ SERVES 4
PREP TIME: 10 MIN
COOK TIME: 15 MIN

1 cup fresh cranberries

1 (8-ounce) can crushed pineapple

2 cups chopped peeled Red Delicious, Empire, or Ambrosia apples

½ teaspoon orange zest

¼ cup fresh orange juice

¼ cup sugar

¼ teaspoon freshly grated nutmeg

1 (8-ounce) package cream cheese, at room temperature

Crackers and pretzels, for serving

One of my favorite things to serve at a party is pepper jelly over cream cheese with crackers. This compote is a sweeter take on a pepper jelly, and everyone enjoys it. Compotes are great because all you need is fruit, water, and sugar. Then you can add whatever else your heart desires. Not only is this recipe great to serve at a party, but it's also tasty as a pick-me-up snack.

1. In a medium pot, combine the cranberries and pineapple and bring to a boil over high heat. Reduce the heat to medium-low and stir in the apples, orange zest, orange juice, sugar, nutmeg, and ¼ cup water. Cook for 8 to 10 minutes, until the apples soften. Using the back of a wooden spoon, smash the apples into small chunks and stir.

2. Place the cream cheese on a serving plate and spoon the compote over the top. Serve with crackers and pretzels for dipping and spreading.

Grape and Pineapple Salsa

1 (8-ounce) can crushed pineapple, drained

1 cup green grapes

3 scallions, chopped

1 teaspoon chopped jalapeño

2 garlic cloves, minced

1 teaspoon sea salt

½ teaspoon ground white pepper

You may have had pineapple in salsa before, but probably not grapes. I use green grapes—they're a bit more sour than red grapes, so go ahead and use red grapes if you want a sweeter salsa. The grapes add just enough sweetness to the salsa and give it a pretty color. You can eat this salsa with tortilla chips, on tacos, and even on grilled meats. The salsa will keep in the refrigerator for up to 1 week.

In a food processor, combine the pineapple, grapes, scallions, jalapeño, garlic, salt, and pepper. Pulse until broken down to your desired consistency. Transfer to a bowl and serve.

Pumpkin-Apple Dip

SERVES 10
PREP TIME: 15 MIN
COOK TIME: 0 MIN

2 (8-ounce) packages cream cheese, at room temperature

1 (15-ounce) can pure pumpkin

1 cup unsweetened applesauce

½ cup packed light brown sugar

1 tablespoon mulling spice, ground

Apples, cored and sliced, for serving

Pretzels, for serving

When I serve this dip, I like to cut the tops off some mini pumpkins and scoop out the insides. I place the dip inside the pumpkins and serve it like that. I made this one day and had so much dip left over that I decided to share it with my friends at school. When lunchtime rolled around and I pulled out the dip from my lunch kit, everyone was amazed at how gorgeous it looked. Once they tasted it, it was gone in seconds!

1. In a large bowl, stir together the cream cheese, pumpkin, applesauce, brown sugar, and mulling spice until creamy and well combined.

2. Serve with apple slices and pretzels for dipping.

Winter

Meyer *Lemon*–Balsamic Braised Chicken

⚜ SERVES 4
PREP TIME: 15 MIN
COOK TIME: 50 MIN

2 tablespoons olive oil

1 pound boneless, skinless chicken thighs, cut into 3-inch pieces (4 ounces each)

2 teaspoons sea salt

1 teaspoon ground black pepper

1 cup thinly sliced yellow onion

1 Meyer lemon, sliced and seeded

2 garlic cloves, minced

1 cup chicken broth

2 tablespoons balsamic vinegar

2 tablespoons pure maple syrup

1½ teaspoons chopped fresh dill, plus more for garnish

1 pound whole-wheat linguine

Meyer lemons are generally sweeter than standard lemons, so I always enjoy eating a piece of Meyer lemon with my chicken and pasta. If you aren't able to find Meyer lemons, you can slice half a regular lemon and half an orange to use in this recipe. That way, you can still have the tanginess of a lemon but the sweetness of an orange in your dish.

1. In a large cast-iron skillet, heat the oil over medium heat. Season the chicken on both sides with the salt and pepper. Add the chicken to the pan and cook for 5 minutes on each side, or until cooked through and golden brown. Transfer the chicken to a large plate and set aside.

2. Add the onion to the pan and cook, stirring occasionally, for 8 to 10 minutes, until the onion begins to brown. Add the Meyer lemon and garlic and cook for 1 minute. Add the broth and stir, scraping up any browned bits from the bottom of the pan with a wooden spoon, then stir in the vinegar, maple syrup, and dill. Return the chicken to the skillet. Reduce the heat to medium-low, cover, and cook for 30 minutes, or until the liquid has reduced by half.

3. Meanwhile, bring a large pot of water to a boil. Add the pasta and cook according to the package directions. Drain and set aside until ready to serve.

4. Serve the chicken over the cooked pasta, garnished with the remaining dill.

Borscht

5 red beets

2 tablespoons olive oil, plus more as needed

1 pound boneless, skinless chicken breasts, chopped

1 yellow onion, chopped

4 garlic cloves, minced

2 cups shredded carrots

1 large potato, peeled and chopped

1 cup shredded cabbage

1 teaspoon smoked paprika

8 cups chicken broth

2 tablespoons cider vinegar

2 teaspoons sea salt

½ teaspoon ground black pepper

Sour cream, for serving

Chopped fresh dill, for garnish

Borscht is a traditional, hearty Ukrainian soup that has the perfect balance of sweet and sour. Roasting brings out the sweetness in the beets, while the vinegar adds a slight tanginess. The soup gets its unique color from the beets, which stain the onion, cabbage, and potatoes as well.

1. Preheat the oven to 400°F.

2. Place the beets on a baking sheet and lightly coat them with oil. Roast for 1 hour, or until fork-tender. Remove from the oven and let cool for 10 minutes. Peel and chop the beets and set aside.

3. In a medium pan, heat 1 tablespoon oil over medium-high heat. Add the chicken and cook for 8 to 10 minutes, until cooked through and golden brown. Set aside.

4. In a large pot, heat the remaining 1 tablespoon oil over medium heat. Add the onion and cook, stirring frequently, for 3 to 5 minutes, until translucent. Stir in the garlic and cook for 30 seconds. Add the carrots, potato, and cabbage and cook for 5 minutes. Add the chopped beets, cooked chicken, paprika, broth, vinegar, salt, and pepper. Increase the heat to high and bring the mixture to a boil. Reduce the heat to low and simmer for 30 minutes, or until reduced by one-fourth.

5. Ladle the borscht into bowls and serve with a dollop of sour cream and garnish with some fresh dill.

Beef Stroganoff with Baby *Carrots*

❧ SERVES 4
PREP TIME: 20 MIN
COOK TIME: 2 HRS 15 MIN

¼ cup all-purpose flour

3 tablespoons seasoning salt

1½ pounds chuck roast, chopped

4 tablespoons olive oil

1 large red onion, chopped

4 garlic cloves, minced

2 cups sliced white button mushrooms

1 cup baby carrots

4 cups beef broth

1 tablespoon Worcestershire sauce

1 teaspoon freshly grated nutmeg

1 pound egg noodles

1 cup 2% Greek yogurt

In this take on a traditional beef stroganoff, the Greek yogurt replaces the sour cream and olive oil is substituted for the butter. This lightens up the dish while still making it creamy. No one will even realize they are eating a healthier version of beef stroganoff because it tastes just as delicious as the original.

1. In a large resealable plastic bag, combine the flour and 1 tablespoon of the seasoning salt and shake until combined. Place the roast in the bag, seal, and shake to coat each piece of meat with the seasoned flour.

2. In a large Dutch oven, heat 2 tablespoons of the oil over medium heat. Add the onion and cook, stirring frequently, for 5 to 7 minutes, until translucent. Stir in the garlic and cook for 30 seconds. Transfer the onion mixture to a bowl and set aside.

3. In the same pot, heat the remaining 2 tablespoons oil over medium-high heat. Add the meat and cook for 7 to 8 minutes, until browned on all sides. Return the onion mixture to the pot and add the mushrooms, carrots, broth, Worcestershire, remaining 2 tablespoons seasoning salt, and nutmeg. Reduce the heat to low, cover, and simmer, stirring occasionally, for 2 hours, or until reduced by half.

4. Meanwhile, bring a large pot of water to a boil. Add the egg noodles and cook according to the package directions. Drain and set aside.

5. Remove the beef from the heat and stir in the yogurt. Serve immediately over the cooked egg noodles.

Brussels Sprout and Beef Soup

SERVES 8
PREP TIME: 20 MIN
COOK TIME: 1 HR 15 MIN

1 tablespoon olive oil

2 pounds top round beef, cut into 1-inch pieces

1 cup chopped yellow onion

¼ cup chopped bell pepper

2 tablespoons Italian seasoning

½ teaspoon ground cumin

3 garlic cloves, minced

2 cups Brussels sprouts, halved

6 small potatoes, chopped

1 (14.5-ounce) can diced tomatoes

6 cups beef broth

1 teaspoon sea salt

1 teaspoon ground white pepper

Because I love Brussels sprouts so much, I decided to grow them in my garden. When they were ready to be harvested, I had *a lot* of Brussels sprouts on the stalk. I needed to make something with them, so I cooked this soup. It was a chilly day, and this was the perfect way to warm up.

In a large pot, heat the oil over medium heat. Add the beef and cook, stirring, for 7 to 8 minutes, until cooked through and browned on all sides. Add the onion, bell pepper, Italian seasoning, and cumin and cook for 5 minutes. Stir in the garlic and cook for 30 seconds. Add the Brussels sprouts, potatoes, tomatoes, broth, salt, and white pepper and cook, stirring occasionally, for 1 hour, until the beef and Brussels sprouts are tender.

Leek and Potato Bisque

3 tablespoons olive oil

2 leeks, white parts only, thoroughly washed and chopped

4 large garlic cloves, minced

4 red potatoes, quartered

2 teaspoons smoked paprika

½ teaspoon fennel seed

1 teaspoon sea salt

½ teaspoon ground white pepper

5 cups vegetable broth

Zest and juice of 2 limes

The lime zest and juice bring a nice brightness to this rich and creamy bisque. I also like to serve my bisque garnished with a lime wedge and thinly sliced fried leeks. The leeks add an amazing crunch!

1. In a large Dutch oven, heat the oil over medium heat. Add the leeks and cook, stirring occasionally, for 15 minutes, until the leeks soften. Add the garlic, potatoes, and paprika and cook for 10 minutes. Add the fennel, salt, and pepper and cook for 5 minutes. Reduce the heat to low and stir in the broth, lime zest, and lime juice. Simmer for 20 minutes.

2. Using an immersion blender, blend the soup directly in the pot until smooth and creamy.

Fried *Leeks*

1 leek

1. Slice the white part of one leek in half and wash it thoroughly. Thinly slice the leek.

2. In a large pan, heat 1 inch of vegetable or canola oil over medium heat until the oil begins to create small bubbles. Carefully drop the leek slices into the hot oil and fry for 10 to 15 seconds, until golden brown.

3. Transfer the leeks to a paper towel–lined plate to drain before using.

Kale Pesto Pasta

1 pound farfalle pasta

1 cup fresh basil

2 cups coarsely chopped kale leaves

½ cup sliced almonds

½ cup grated Parmesan cheese

1 teaspoon minced garlic

1 teaspoon sea salt

½ teaspoon ground black pepper

¼ cup olive oil

1 cup vegetable broth

I love adding greens, whether it's kale, spinach, or other herbs, to supplement some basil in my pesto. Although kale can sometimes have a bitter taste, the basil helps to add some sweetness. I also use vegetable broth in place of some of the olive oil to make the pesto lighter while still keeping it flavorful.

1. Bring a large pot of water to a boil. Add the pasta and cook according to the package directions. Drain and set aside.

2. Meanwhile, bring a separate large pot of water to a boil. Fill a large bowl with ice and water and set it nearby. Add the kale to the boiling water and cook for 2 to 3 minutes. Drain and transfer to the ice bath. Let cool, then drain again and set aside.

3. In a food processor, combine the basil, blanched kale, almonds, cheese, garlic, salt, pepper, and oil. Process until well combined. With the motor running, gradually stream the broth through the feed tube, stopping occasionally to scrape down the sides with a spatula, until the pesto is smooth.

4. Stir the pesto into the cooked pasta and serve.

Sesame-Peanut Noodles

❖ SERVES 6
PREP TIME: 10 MIN
COOK TIME: 10 MIN

1 pound whole-wheat angel hair pasta

3 tablespoons creamy peanut butter

1 tablespoon toasted sesame oil

1 teaspoon soy sauce

½ cup fresh orange juice

2 teaspoons grated fresh ginger

1 tablespoon chopped fresh mint

1 tablespoon chopped fresh parsley

Whenever my mom and I would order spring rolls at a restaurant, she would dip them in *nuớc chấm*, a savory sauce made with lime juice, sugar, and nam pla (fish sauce). I love dipping them in the sweet peanut sauce and scraping up whatever's left in the bowl. I decided to make my own version of the peanut sauce to mix with pasta, and wow, it's good!

1. Bring a large pot of water to a boil. Add the pasta and cook according to the package directions. Drain and set aside.

2. In a small jar with a lid, combine the peanut butter, oil, soy sauce, orange juice, and ginger. Cover and shake until well combined.

3. Add the sauce to the cooked pasta and toss to coat. Mix in the mint and parsley and serve.

Smashed *Rutabaga*

✦ SERVES 4
PREP TIME: 10 MIN
COOK TIME: 35 MIN

2 large rutabagas, peeled and cut into 1-inch chunks

1 teaspoon olive oil

1 teaspoon minced garlic

2 teaspoons honey

1 cup heavy cream

1 teaspoon sea salt

1 tablespoon finely chopped fresh dill

This alternative to your traditional mashed potatoes uses rutabagas in place of the potatoes. I smash the rutabagas, leaving some chunks intact, because I like the texture. In this dish you can taste the fresh, bright dill and sweet honey first, followed by a slightly sweet, earthy flavor from the rutabagas.

1. Bring a large pot of water to a boil. Add the rutabaga and cook for 30 minutes, or until fork-tender, then drain.

2. In the same pot, heat the oil over medium heat. Add the garlic and cook for 30 seconds. Add the rutabaga and smash it with a potato masher, leaving small chunks intact. Add the honey, cream, salt, and dill. Beat with a handheld mixer until thoroughly combined.

Cream of Roasted *Turnip* Soup

2 turnips, peeled and chopped

2 tablespoons olive oil

3 shallots, finely chopped

2 garlic cloves, minced

2 cups vegetable broth

½ cup whole milk

1 teaspoon grated fresh ginger

1 teaspoon sea salt

1 teaspoon ground white pepper

Once, at my local farmer's market in New Orleans, one of the farmers had a surplus of turnips, so he gave me a bunch. He told me that his favorite way to eat them was when his wife roasted them. I took it one step further and created a creamy roasted turnip soup. It is perfect for beating the cold winter blues.

1. Preheat the oven to 350°F. Line a baking sheet with aluminum foil.

2. Place the turnips on the prepared baking sheet and drizzle with 1 tablespoon of the oil. Toss to coat the turnips with the oil. Roast for 30 to 35 minutes, until fork-tender.

3. In a medium pot, heat the remaining 1 tablespoon oil over medium heat. Add the shallots and cook, stirring frequently, for 3 to 5 minutes, until translucent. Add the broth, milk, ginger, salt, and pepper and stir to combine. Increase the heat to high and bring the mixture to a boil. Reduce the heat to low.

4. Using an immersion blender, blend the soup directly in the pot until creamy and smooth. Serve immediately.

Roasted Lemon-Parsley
Parsnips

4 parsnips, peeled, halved lengthwise, and cut into 1-inch chunks

2 tablespoons olive oil

1 teaspoon minced garlic

1 tablespoon fresh lemon juice

1 tablespoon chopped fresh parsley, plus more for garnish

1 teaspoon sea salt

Pinch of ground black pepper

1 lemon, halved

Parsnips have a subtle but distinctly different flavor than their carrot cousins. A bit spicy when raw, they turn sort of nutty when roasted, whereas carrots are much sweeter. The fresh lemon juice squeezed over the parsnips at the end adds the perfect amount of acidity to the dish.

1. Preheat the oven to 400°F. Line a baking sheet with aluminum foil.

2. In a medium bowl, toss together the parsnips, oil, garlic, lemon juice, parsley, salt, and pepper. Spread the parsnips over the prepared baking sheet. Roast for 20 minutes, or until fork-tender and golden brown.

3. Squeeze the lemon over the parsnips and garnish with more parsley.

Herb-Crusted Pork Roast with *Potatoes* with Carrots and *Potatoes*

⚜ SERVES 4
PREP TIME: 20 MIN
COOK TIME: 5 HRS 15 MIN

½ cup chopped fresh parsley

¼ cup chopped fresh oregano

¼ cup chopped fresh basil

1 yellow onion, chopped

10 garlic cloves

¼ cup olive oil

1 teaspoon sea salt

½ teaspoon ground black pepper

1 (2-pound) pork tenderloin

1 cup chicken broth

1 pound baby carrots

6 red potatoes, quartered

This pork roast is great for meals over the weekend because it takes a bit longer to make. Start cooking it around lunchtime, and it will be ready to eat for dinner. By cooking the pork tenderloin low and slow, you'll end up with tender, juicy meat. The potatoes will soak up the yummy juices and take on that delicious flavor. Mmmm!

1. Preheat the oven to 350°F.

2. In a food processor, combine the parsley, oregano, basil, half the onion, 3 of the garlic cloves, oil, salt, and pepper and process until smooth.

3. Cut 7 (½-inch) slits into the pork and stuff the remaining garlic into the slits. Coat the pork tenderloin with the herb paste.

4. Put the remaining onion and the broth in a large roasting pan and place the coated pork on top of the onion. Cover the pan with aluminum foil and roast for 4 hours. Lift the foil, add the carrots and potatoes to the pan, and re-cover the pan. Roast for 1 hour more, then increase the oven temperature to 400°F, uncover the pan, and roast for 15 minutes, or until the herb paste becomes slightly crispy.

Smoky Roasted *Pumpkin* Bisque

1 (1-pound) pie pumpkin, peeled, seeded, and chopped (4 cups)

4 tablespoons olive oil

1 cup chopped yellow onion

4 garlic cloves, sliced

1 tablespoon paprika

1 tablespoon sea salt

1 teaspoon ground white pepper

1 teaspoon ground cinnamon

1 teaspoon freshly grated nutmeg

4 cups chicken broth

1 tablespoon honey

2 cups grated smoked Gruyère cheese

½ cup heavy cream

Like the pork roast opposite, this bisque is a great weekend dish since it's a bit more time-consuming. It's also perfect for a frigid winter day. Roasting the pumpkin brings out its sweetness. The smoky Gruyère is fabulous when paired with the roasted pumpkin, and I absolutely love creamy bisques!

1. Preheat the oven to 400°F. Line a baking sheet with aluminum foil.

2. Place the pumpkin on the prepared baking sheet and drizzle it with 2 tablespoons of the oil. Toss to coat the pumpkin with the oil. Roast for 40 minutes, or until fork-tender.

3. In a large pot, heat the remaining 2 tablespoons oil over medium heat. Add the onion and cook, stirring frequently, for 3 to 5 minutes, until translucent. Stir in the garlic and cook for 30 seconds. Add the roasted pumpkin, paprika, salt, pepper, cinnamon, and nutmeg and stir to combine. Stir in the broth.

4. Using an immersion blender, blend the mixture directly in the pot until smooth. Stir in the honey, cheese, and cream, reduce the heat to medium-low, and simmer for 20 minutes, or until the cheese has completely melted into the bisque.

Sweet Potato and Jalapeño Cakes

1 sweet potato, peeled and grated

1 large potato, grated

1 jalapeño, seeded and chopped

¼ cup all-purpose flour

1 large egg, beaten

1 tablespoon chopped fresh oregano

¼ cup finely chopped yellow onion

1 large garlic clove, minced

½ teaspoon smoked paprika

1 teaspoon sea salt

½ teaspoon ground black pepper

¼ cup canola oil

This recipe is my take on latkes. Standard latkes are made with potatoes, but I decided to substitute half of the potatoes with sweet potatoes. They add just the right amount of sweetness to balance out the jalapeño. The sugar content in the sweet potatoes also helps brown the cakes quicker.

1. Spread the grated sweet potato and potato on a large microwave-safe plate and microwave for 3 minutes on high.

2. In a large bowl, stir together the sweet potato, potato, jalapeño, flour, egg, oregano, onion, garlic, paprika, salt, and pepper. Form the mixture into 4 small patties.

3. In a large skillet, heat the oil over medium heat. Add the patties and fry for 2 to 3 minutes on each side, until golden brown. Transfer the patties to a paper towel–lined plate to drain before serving.

Pomegranate and Citrus Salad

3 mandarin oranges, peeled and segmented

6 kumquats, quartered and seeded

½ cup pomegranate arils

½ cup canned crushed pineapple

2 tablespoons pineapple juice (reserved from the crushed pineapple)

2 tablespoons honey

Why eat a boring, standard fruit salad when you can switch it up and eat this one? This combination of fruits is the perfect way to brighten up your day. The citrus is like the orange backdrop of a sunset while the pomegranate peeks through with its bold color. Not only is it beautiful, but it's tasty.

In a large bowl, gently stir together the orange, kumquat, pomegranate arils, pineapple, pineapple juice, and honey. Serve immediately.

Pomelo-Coconut Salad

1 pomelo, peeled, chopped, and seeded

2 oranges, peeled, segmented, and seeded

1 cup grapes

¼ cup fresh pomelo juice

2 tablespoons honey

1 tablespoon packed light brown sugar

2 tablespoons full-fat coconut milk

1 tablespoon unsweetened coconut flakes

My nana came over to my house one day with three giant pomelos. I'd never seen them before, so she explained that they're similar to grapefruit. They have a slightly sweeter flavor than grapefruit, though, and are bigger, with a much thicker rind. Because I had so many pomelos, I wanted to create a dish with them instead of just eating them on their own. This winter fruit salad, laced with honey and sprinkled with coconut, makes a wonderful healthy breakfast or dessert.

1. In a large bowl, combine the pomelo, orange, and grapes.

2. In a small bowl, whisk together the pomelo juice, honey, sugar, and coconut milk. Pour the liquid over the fruit and sprinkle the coconut flakes on top before serving. Serve immediately.

Stuffed Butternut *Squash*

2 butternut squash, cut in half lengthwise and seeded

1 tablespoon olive oil, plus more for drizzling

Salt and ground black pepper

½ cup chopped yellow onion

1 tablespoon minced garlic

½ pound frozen vegan ground beef, thawed

1 (15.5-ounce) can chickpeas, rinsed and drained

1 teaspoon garlic powder

1 teaspoon ground dried basil

1 teaspoon ground dried oregano

¼ cup shredded vegan cheddar cheese

When my sister came into town and stayed with us for a bit, she bought vegan ground beef for us to try because she wanted us to see that it tasted like regular ground beef. She asked me to make a meal using the vegan ground beef, and this is what I came up with. The butternut squash is so tender when roasted. I love that this stuffed squash is a meal in itself, and it is so good!

1. Preheat the oven to 400°F. Line a rimmed baking sheet with aluminum foil.

2. Score the flesh of the butternut squash in a crosshatch pattern to make ½-inch pieces. Place the squash on the prepared baking sheet and drizzle with oil and sprinkle each half with a pinch each of salt and pepper. Roast for 1 hour, until fork-tender.

3. In a large pan, heat the oil over medium heat. Add the onion and cook, stirring frequently, for 3 to 5 minutes, until translucent. Stir in the garlic and cook for 30 seconds. Add the vegan ground beef and cook, stirring, for 8 to 10 minutes, until heated through. Add the chickpeas, garlic powder, basil, and oregano and stir to combine.

4. Scoop the roasted squash flesh out of the skins, leaving about ¼ inch attached to the skins so the shells hold their shape; return the squash shells to the baking sheet and set aside. Add the flesh to the pan with the vegan beef mixture and stir to combine.

5. Stuff the squash shells with the vegan beef mixture. Sprinkle the cheese on top of the stuffing, dividing it evenly. Bake for 5 minutes, or until the cheese has melted. Serve immediately.

Pear Tart

⚜ SERVES 6
PREP TIME: 1 HR 40 MIN
COOK TIME: 15 MIN

1 frozen puff pastry sheet, thawed

1 tablespoon unsalted butter, melted

2 medium pears, cored and cut into ¼-inch-thick slices

2 teaspoons fresh lemon juice

1 tablespoon sugar

¼ teaspoon ground cinnamon

I love how the cinnamon adds warmth to the tart while the sugar caramelizes and sweetens the pears. When making this pear tart, you can add any other seasonal fruit, such as apples or pineapples. You can even use a combination of fruits.

1. Preheat the oven to 400°F. Line a baking sheet with parchment paper.

2. Place the puff pastry sheet on the prepared baking sheet. Fold the edges of the puff pastry over ½ inch. Brush the entire surface of the puff pastry with the melted butter. Using a fork, poke holes in the puff pastry (do not poke the folded-over border). Layer the pear slices in two rows on the puff pastry. Drizzle the lemon juice over the pears.

3. In a small bowl, mix together the sugar and cinnamon. Evenly sprinkle the cinnamon-sugar over the pears. Bake for 15 minutes, or until puff pastry is cooked through and golden brown.

Pear Tart
PAGE 149

Banana-Coconut Bread

❧ SERVES 8

PREP TIME: 10 MIN
COOK TIME: 1 HR 15 MIN

Nonstick cooking spray

1¼ cups sugar

½ cup (1 stick) unsalted butter,
at room temperature

2 large eggs

4 overripe bananas, mashed

1 cup unsweetened coconut flakes

½ cup full-fat coconut milk

½ cup coconut cream

2½ cups self-rising flour, or 2½ cups
all-purpose flour plus 3¼ teaspoons
baking powder

1 teaspoon sea salt

1 cup chopped almonds (optional)

Replacing dairy milk with coconut milk adds a lovely tropical flavor to this bread. I could eat banana bread every day, so if you're anything like me, you might want to make an extra loaf for yourself. And don't forget to hide it, or someone might eat it when you're not looking!

1. Preheat the oven to 350°F. Grease a 9 x 5-inch loaf pan with cooking spray.

2. In a large bowl, stir together the sugar and butter. Whisk in the eggs. Mix in the bananas, coconut flakes, coconut milk, and coconut cream. Add the flour and salt and stir until they are incorporated. Fold in the almonds (if using).

3. Pour the batter into the prepared loaf pan and bake for 1 hour 15 minutes, or until a toothpick inserted into the center of the bread comes out clean. Let cool for 10 minutes before serving. Once completely cooled, store in an airtight container or wrap with plastic wrap. It will stay fresh for up to 2 days when stored at room temperature and up to 1 week when in the refrigerator.

Kumquat Muffins

⚜ SERVES 12
PREP TIME: 20 MIN
COOK TIME: 20 MIN

½ cup granulated sugar

¼ cup packed light brown sugar

2 large eggs

¼ cup coconut oil, melted

1 cup fresh orange juice
(from 3 or 4 oranges)

10 kumquats, seeded

1 cup self-rising flour, or 1 cup
all-purpose flour plus 1¼ teaspoons
baking powder

½ cup whole-wheat pastry flour

1 teaspoon baking soda

Pinch of sea salt

Kumquats are a great citrus alternative to oranges and tangerines. The good thing about kumquats is that you don't have to peel them because you can eat their skins. They have a bit of a sour tanginess, so using them in muffins brings out their sweetness.

1. Preheat the oven to 350°F. Line a muffin tin with 12 paper liners.

2. In a large bowl, whisk together the granulated sugar, brown sugar, eggs, and melted coconut oil until well combined.

3. In a food processor, combine the orange juice and kumquats and purée.

4. Add the kumquat mixture to the bowl with the sugar mixture and stir to combine. Stir in the self-rising flour, pastry flour, baking soda, and salt.

5. Scoop ¼ cup of the batter into each well of the prepared muffin tin. Bake for 17 to 20 minutes, until a toothpick inserted into the center of a muffin comes out clean. Once completely cooled, store in an airtight container at room temperature for up to 3 days.

Inside-Out *Apple* Pie

6 tablespoons unsalted butter

3 apples, cored and chopped (3 cups)

½ cup packed light brown sugar

½ teaspoon ground cinnamon

½ teaspoon freshly grated nutmeg

½ teaspoon pure vanilla extract

Pinch of sea salt

½ cup chopped pecans

1 (8-ounce) package frozen phyllo dough, thawed

This is "inside out" because the apple filling is on the outside instead of being covered with a crust. Although preparing the phyllo dough can be a bit time-consuming, it is definitely worth it. You end up with a flaky, buttery bottom crust and warm, sweet apple filling. Talk about delish!

1. Preheat the oven to 350°F.

2. In a large pot, melt 2 tablespoons of the butter over medium heat. Add the apples, sugar, cinnamon, nutmeg, vanilla, and salt and cook, stirring occasionally, for 5 minutes, until apples begin to soften. Remove from the heat and stir in the pecans.

3. Place the remaining butter in a microwave-safe bowl and microwave for 30 seconds to 1 minute, until melted. Lay out a sheet of phyllo dough and brush it with melted butter. Top it with another sheet of phyllo dough and repeat until all the phyllo dough is layered and buttered.

4. Cut the phyllo dough into eight equal rectangles. Use the phyllo dough rectangles to line eight wells of a muffin tin, pushing the dough into the edges of the wells, and fill them with the filling. Bake for 25 minutes, until the phyllo dough is cooked through and golden brown.

Acknowledgments

THANK YOU TO EVERYONE WHO HAS
SUPPORTED MY DREAMS:

Chef Frank Brigtsen

Airielle Brooks

Dad (Antonio Casas)

Guisela Casas and family

Abuela (Jennie Casas)

Demetris Chambliss Jr.

Paw Paw (Clay Chretien)

Nana (Josie Chretien)

Gianna Collura

Mom (Dianne de Las Casas)

Gia Herring

Ashlynn James

Camrynn James

Uncle Gary (Gary James)

Jasmynn James

Soleil Lisette

Chef Dana Tuohy

Chef Jessie Wightkin-Gelini

Khalilah Williams

Reagan Williams

Index

Note: Page references in *italics* indicate photographs.